# *Along the* RIVER CAM

ANDREW HUNTER BLAIR

SUTTON PUBLISHING

First published in the United Kingdom in 2007
Sutton Publishing Limited · Phoenix Mill
Thrupp · Stroud · Gloucestershire · GL5 2BU

British Library Cataloguing in Publication Data
A catalogue record for this book is available from the British Library.

ISBN 978-0-7509-4455-7

*In Memory of Archie Buchanan*

Typeset in 10.5/13pt Galliard.
Typesetting and origination by
Sutton Publishing Limited.
Printed and bound in England.

# Contents

# About the Author

Andrew Hunter Blair is a chartered civil engineer who was educated at Rugby School and Queen's University, Belfast, where he gained a BSc and MSc. After a short spell at the Great Ouse River Board in Cambridge he spent nine years at the Water Research Association at Medmenham on the Thames. Here he pioneered work on underground water and presented many papers at national and international conferences. In 1974 he returned to East Anglia where he joined Anglian Water at its new headquarters in Huntingdon to work on fluvial and tidal aspects of water management. On its formation he continued this work at the Anglian Region headquarters of the National Rivers Authority in Peterborough. He retired from his post as Regional Coordinator in December 1993 after which he undertook consultancy work for Northumbrian Water, Sir William Halcrow & Partners and the Middle Level Commissioners. He is a Liveryman of the Worshipful Company of Plumbers and a Freeman of the City of London.

Latterly Andrew has expressed his knowledge and love of the East Anglian rivers and the Fens in two practical and popular publications, namely *The River Great Ouse and Tributaries, A Guide for River Users*, and *Fenland Waterways. A Map and Commentary of the Waterways of the Middle Level*. Two further publications, *Great Ouse Country* and *A Level Country*, are anecdotal sketches of riverside and fenland, folk and history respectively.

All the photographs in this book were taken by the author.

# Acknowledgements

The author gratefully acknowledges all the assistance he has received from those he has met along the river banks and in the riverside villages, including Peter Garner of Guilden Morden Hall and Henry King of Chesterford Mill. Particular mention should be made of the many Cambridge University and College officials for their kindness in giving access to photographs and for their interest. Thanks are due to former colleagues at the Environment Agency and the River Cam Conservancy. Above all thanks are due to all at Sutton Publishing and especially to Simon Fletcher and Clare Jackson, without whose guidance this book would not have been possible.

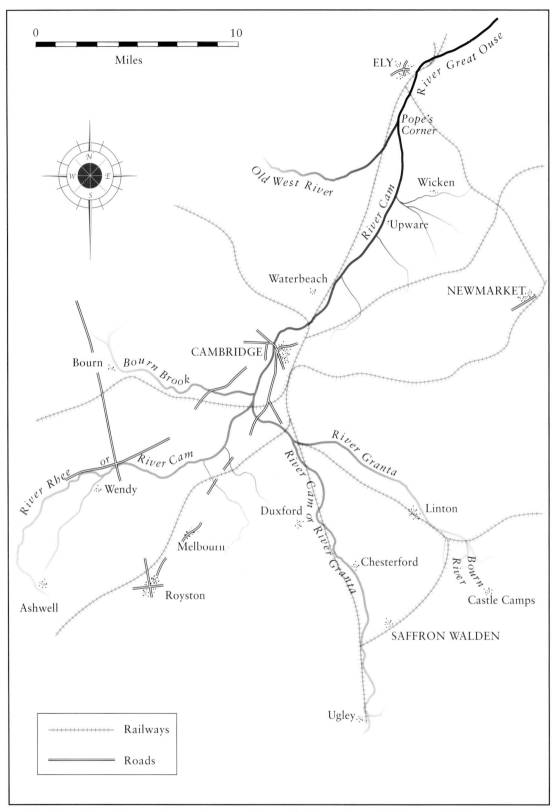

*The River Cam, Rhee or Granta (based on George Philip & Son in J. Murray, 1892).*

# *Introduction*

## CAM, RHEE OR GRANTA, CALL IT AS YOU PLEASE

This is the anecdotal story of the River Cam or 'Cam, Rhee or Granta, call it as you please' (adapted from Thomas Fuller *c*. 1655). Many rivers in Cambridgeshire have a disconcerting trait of changing or duplicating their names and the rivers that form the River Cam are no exception. They could be likened to the four fingers and thumb of a left hand, the palm of the hand being Byron's Pool. To the west, the little finger is the Bourn Brook. Moving east, according to the Ordnance Survey, is the River Cam or Rhee, sometimes known as the Ashwell Cam, after its source. For clarity in *Along the River Cam* this river, the ring finger, will be called the River Rhee. Both the Bourn Brook and the River Rhee cut across the western clay plateau forming a broad valley. The middle finger, again according to the Ordnance Survey, is the River Cam or Granta, sometimes known as the Saffron Walden Cam. It would be fitting that this longest branch be known simply as the River Cam. Moving further east to the next branch or index finger is the relatively short River Granta, sometimes called the Linton Cam or even the River Bourn. To avoid confusion it will be called the River Granta. Both these rivers rise in upland boulder clay on the borders of Hertfordshire, Essex and Cambridgeshire and quickly cut through into the upper, middle and lower chalk bands. The thumb can represent the very short Bourn River.

As they derive their base flow from the underground chalk water, during droughts or prolonged dry spells their flow, particularly during the summer, can be very low. Indeed, in their upper reaches the word 'river' or 'brook' can seem to be somewhat of an exaggeration. The flow comes and goes and frequently the bed of the river will be dry or there is a barely discernible glimpse of water between overgrown banks.

All these rivers will have joined and gained in stature by the time they reach Byron's Pool, and it is confusing that between this pool and Silver Street Bridge they should be collectively known locally as the River Granta as opposed to the River Cam, the Ordnance Survey definition. In part this confusion will have arisen from the old names for the River Cam, Cambridge and Grantchester. The early name for Cambridge was Grantabridge (Bridge over the Granta). By 1086 this had evolved to Cantabridge and then corrupted to Cambridge, Bridge over the Cam. Grantchester originated from Granteseta, that is, 'Settlers by the Granta'. There is no confusion after Silver Street Bridge; the rivers above Cambridge, once described as ditches, have now become the River Cam, once described below Cambridge as a sewer. Both descriptions are totally unfair today.

The River Cam flows under Silver Street Bridge past 'The Backs' of the famous Cambridge colleges – Queens', King's, Clare, Trinity Hall, Trinity and St John's – to Bridge Street and Magdalene College. Leaving Cambridge towards the Fens, now assuming a single identity, the Cam's character changes subtly from a meandering upland river to one that is straight, embanked and sometimes artificial. It became part of a Roman waterway between Cambridge and Lincoln and formed the boundary of, successively, a republic and a kingdom. It became a navigable commercial river with locks and a 'haling' (hauling) way, a popular cruising river, a racecourse and a means of conveying floodwaters from the Fens. It meets Roman canals called Lodes. Finally at Pope's Corner, in sight of Ely Cathedral, the great Ship of the Fens, and some 40 miles from its source, it joins the Old West River. Their combined names change to the River Great Ouse or Ely Ouse that carries their waters a further 35½ miles to the sea at King's Lynn.

Initially the rivers flow through quintessential English countryside and villages, often set in pairs on either bank with names such as Ugley, Wendons Ambo, Castle Camps and Abingdon Piggots. Along their way they pass ancient churches, abbeys and country houses, great and small, including Audley End House, Wimpole Hall, Sawston Hall, Morden Hall, Down Hall, Denny Abbey and Anglesey Abbey. They discover warplanes, radio telescopes, agro-chemicals, synthetic resins, plant breeders, leather and tanning, and the human genome. They meet gods, saints and sinners, kings and queens, presidents, bishops, abbots and priors, dukes and duchesses, counts and countesses, knights and heroes, tyrants, oppressors and murderers, academics, poets and inventors, citizens, landowners and farmers, and demons and ghosts.

All of these are to be found along the River Cam.

# 1

# *The River Cam in Essex*

The most southerly tributary of the River Cam rises in boulder clay uplands near Henham in Essex, the long winding street of which forms the watershed between upper tributaries of the Rivers Cam, Stort and Chelmer. In its church, with its 'Hertfordshire Spike' and fearsome gargoyles that include one of a little man crouching with his head between his knees on his journey to Hell, is a memorial to Samuel Feake (1790), one-time governor of Fort William in Calcutta.

However if the true source of a river is judged to be the river's furthest point from the sea as the fish swims, then the source of the River Cam lies between the Domesday Manor of Amberden Hall and Mole Hall, an Elizabethan hall house and now a small wildlife park. While Henham and Amberden are connected by water, they were once connected by the Elsenham and Thaxted Light Railway which ran along the watershed between the Rivers Cam and Chelmer. Having been granted a Light Railway Order in 1906, construction, which started in 1911, was completed in 1918. Typical of many light railways, with its elderly rolling stock, slow service, minimal facilities and few passengers, it closed for passengers in 1952 and was completely closed in 1953.

The small stream meets the Henham tributary between Henham and Ugley, Ugga's Glade. Possibly a corruption of Oakley, the village belies its name and its Women's Institute must be tired of quips about its title. Ugley Hall dates from the sixteenth century and the church's Tudor brick tower is said to have been the last in Essex to house pigeons.

Now the small river turns north into the Cam valley where it is paralleled by the Cambridge to London Liverpool Street railway line, the former A11 now the B1383, and, a short distance to the west, the M11 motorway. Initially the valley runs in glacial sands and gravels that overlie boulder clay, which in turn overlies the upper chalk. In its lower reaches it runs in valley gravels; the boulder clay retreats and the upper, middle and lower chalk become exposed. Although the valley has now become part of the M11 corridor and is close to Stansted Airport, the catchment remains largely arable and almost totally devoted to agriculture.

In a similar manner to the Rivers Rhee and Granta valleys, a railway line was built along the River Cam valley. Unlike those in the Rhee and Granta valleys, it survives. This railway line, from Cambridge to London, was initially a project of the Northern and Eastern Railway which, after many difficulties, opened up the line as far as Broxbourne in 1840 and shortly afterwards to Bishop's Stortford. Here its money ran out and the company was leased in 1844 by the Eastern Counties Railway which completed the line to Cambridge in 1847. Soon after, however, this company too fell into financial difficulties; its locomotives and rolling stock were seized and it was declared bankrupt. In 1862 it was amalgamated into the Great Eastern Railway, which went on to become a part of the London and North Eastern Railway.

In its early days the line had a poor reputation. Passengers could not rely on being carried to their destination without delays, not of minutes, but of hours. Frequently trains failed to arrive at their destination and returned to their starting point. According to *Punch*, 'On Wednesday last a respectably dressed young man was seen to go to the Shoreditch terminus of the Eastern Counties Railway and deliberately take a ticket for Cambridge. He has not been heard of since. No motive has been assigned for this rash act.' While a number of express trains, including 'The Fenman', took this route, the emphasis changed in 1932 when the London and North Eastern Railway introduced 'The Garden Cities and Cambridge Buffet Express', which ran to London five times a day via the slightly longer route to King's Cross. The twisty line remains the slower route to London.

The river continues north towards Newport passing Quendon to the west and to the east Widdington. Quendon Hall and Quendon Court date from about 1540 and

*The Crown House at Newport.*

about 1750 respectively. Thomas and William Winstanley, father and uncle to Henry Winstanley (of Littlebury and builder of the Eddystone lighthouse) were reportedly buried in wool, a form of burial used, among other things, at Quendon between 1621 and 1792. William is believed to have started his career as a London barber before becoming famous for his popular 'Poor Robin' almanacs and chapbooks. Widdington's Prior's Hall Barn, possibly based on a thirteenth-century stone house, comprises one of the finest preserved fifteenth-century timber-framed barns in the country and is an English Heritage site.

Newport, far from any river that could sustain a port, is the first village of any significant size through which the River Cam flows. While its ancient market was removed north to Saffron Walden, its fair continued. According to thirteenth-century records there were glovers, grocers, furriers, carpenters, vintners, coopers, dyers, goldsmiths and a moneylender (listed in Scarfe). A number of fine ancient buildings include the Crown House, named after its pargeted crown shown in high relief and below which is a large shell hood above the door the lintel of which carries the date 1692. The house is earlier than the date suggests, possibly late sixteenth or early seventeenth century. It was previously the Horns Inn where Nell Gwyn is alleged to have stayed on her way to visit the king in Newmarket. Other noteworthy houses include a fifteenth-century range (The Priory), now cottages, with their original oriel windows abutting the railway bridge, the former House of Correction, appropriately called The Links with elegantly carved shackles on its white Georgian front, and Monks Barn, half timbered like a Kentish hall house with a projecting oriel window below which are carved figures of the Virgin and Child being entertained by angels playing harp and organ. Although the buildings of the former grammar school are mainly mid-Victorian but built in the style of Charles I, it was first an Elizabethan foundation by 'a bereaved lady who thus gained twenty good sons to comfort her for the loss of one' (quotation in Scarfe). It was the school of Jocosa (Joyce) Frankland (née Trappes, 1531–87), founder of the Saxey fellowships and scholarships at Caius and Emmanuel Colleges in Cambridge and benefactor to Lincoln and Brasenose Colleges in Oxford.

At the north end of the village is a large erratic reddish-brown sandstone called 'The Leper's Stone'. It is supposed to have been the stone in whose cavities coins were placed as an offering in return for food set down there by the brethren of the nearby Leper's Hospital. Its association with charity could be much earlier since it may have been a meeting place where 'obligations were satisfied by the usual Pagan invocations to their Gods with offerings of food and libations which afterwards became the portion of the poor' (quotation in Warren). It was said to have been blown over during a severe storm at the end of the eighteenth century to the great concern of all the inhabitants who regarded the event as a bad omen.

The original hospital probably lay to the north since pillars of its chapel are incorporated in the walls of Shortgrove Park. Built by Giles Dent in the mid-seventeenth century with wings added by the Earl of Thomond (O'Brien) at the end of the seventeenth century, it was gutted by fire in 1966 while being converted into a hotel. In the thirteenth-century church, which was in all likelihood associated with the hospital, is a rare thirteenth-century wooden portable altar, sometimes used as a Communion table. With its lid raised four portraits – of the Virgin and three saints – are displayed.

Debden Water and Wicken Water join the River Cam at Newport from the east and west respectively. While the potential of the upper reaches of Debden Water, the 'Deep Dene', was first recognised by its Norman owner Ranulf Peverel, who planted vines, it was landscaped, possibly by Humphry Repton (1752–1818), to form a park with lakes, a bridge and a waterfall. The hall, destroyed in 1935, was bought by Richard Chiswell the Younger (1673–1731) in 1715. Not only was he MP for Calne, but he was also a merchant of Turkish goods and travelled much in the East. His father, Richard Chiswell the Elder (1639–1711), was a London bookseller and publisher at the Rose and Crown in St Paul's churchyard.

Wicken Water rises near Duddenhoe End with its timber and thatched church, looking to all intents and purposes like a barn, and flows through Arkesden, the sixteenth-century home of the Cutte family. In the church is the tomb of Richard Cutte and his wife. He claims descent from Henry VIII's treasurer and the builder of Horham Hall near Thaxted, while she claims to have been the daughter of Edward Erlington, the chief butler to Edward VI and Queen Elizabeth I. The son of another later Richard Cutte was known as John Cutts. Born in Arkesden in 1661, he was nicknamed Salamander and was a hero of Macaulay. He was first and foremost a soldier who served with the Duke of Marlborough, fought for William III at the Battle of the Boyne and led the attack at the Battle of Blenheim in 1704. He was created Baron Cutts of Gowran in Ireland (1690) and was MP for Cambridgeshire and Newport, simultaneously holding the post of Commander-in-Chief in Ireland. He died in Dublin in 1707. Wicken Bonhunt lies between Arkesden and Newport; Brick House, the early home of the Bradbury family dates from about 1600 and includes carved gables of about 1660. To the east, almost swamped by the M11, are the remains of the early Norman chapel of St Helen.

The neighbouring parishes of Great (Magna) and Little (Parva) Wenden lie about 1 mile south of Newport and amalgamated in 1662 to form the village of Wendens Ambo, 'Both Wendens'. The church at Little Wenden was abandoned and demolished; the church of St Mary the Virgin at Great Wenden became established as the principal church. With early Norman or possibly Saxon remains, medieval murals illustrate the life of St Margaret of Antioch. In its churchyard is the tomb of one William Nicholson who was a midshipman on Nelson's ship *Vanguard*; he died aged 104. The main street, with its ancient barns and individual colour-washed houses and cottages, justifiably claims to be one of the finest in Essex. Its railway station, opened in 1845 and called Wendon, is now incongruously called Audley End, a commuter station some distance from Audley End House, and formerly at the start of the line to Saffron Walden and Bartlow. Before its closure in 1964 the motive power was a diesel rail-bus that had succeeded the 1950s 'push-pull' steam train with its two old brown pre-clerestory express coaches dating from the late nineteenth century.

Audley End House and its lands lie on the site of a Benedictine priory founded in 1136 by Geoffrey de Mandeville, 1st Earl of Essex. Situated at 'the confluence of two streams and meeting of four roads, for the convenience of the poor and of travellers' (quotation in Scarfe), it was elevated to an abbey in 1190. Shortly after its dissolution Henry VIII granted the lands and buildings in 1538 to Sir Thomas Audley. Nothing now remains of the original abbey except the mill race and, possibly, the stables. Sir Thomas Audley (1488–1544), Baron Audley of Walden, was both the speaker of the parliament which had decreed the dissolution of the lesser religious houses and, later, the lord chancellor who greatly assisted Henry VIII in the dissolution of the greater religious houses. He was keen to acquire monastic spoils, and while he was still Speaker received the Priory of Christchurch, Aldgate, 'the first cut in the feast of abbey lands, and, I assure you, a dainty morsel'. He also obtained St Botolph's Priory, the Priory of Crutched Friars, both in Colchester, and Tiltey Abbey near Thaxted.

While Thomas may not have actually lived at Audley End, the estate passed on via his daughter Margaret. Aged only fourteen, she married Lord Henry Dudley (1531?–57). After his death at the Battle of St Quentin she became the second wife of Thomas Howard, 4th Duke of Norfolk (1536–72). She died aged twenty-three in

*Audley End House.*

1563. The duke, after marrying again and losing a third wife, was beheaded for his part in the conspiracy to put Mary Queen of Scots on the throne. After his death, although his younger brother, Lord Henry Howard, later the Earl of Northampton, lived at Audley End, the estate was restored in 1582 to the duke's son, and Thomas Audley's grandson, Thomas Howard (1561–1626), 1st Earl of Suffolk and 1st Baron Howard of Walden.

Having distinguished himself against the Armada and been an admiral of the third squadron in the Cadiz expedition, he was, between 1614 and 1618, lord high treasurer. It was he who between 1610 and 1614 rebuilt the mansion, possibly to an Italian design by John Thorpe (fl. 1570–1610) and with the assistance of stonemason Bernard Janssen (d. 1630) at a reported cost of £200,000. At the time it was the largest, most stately and most palatial house in England and was said by James I to be 'too large for a king, though it might do for a Lord Treasurer'. The design comprised two large courtyards. The larger western one was approached by a bridge across the River Cam and through a double avenue of lime trees and a gatehouse. Three sides of this courtyard consisted of apartments supported on alabaster pillars above open cloisters. On the fourth, eastern side, steps led to a terrace and the principal mansion. An inner courtyard lay beyond, with two-storey ranges and its eastern side being formed by a long gallery.

To finance the construction, both the earl and particularly his wife sold other property, and indeed it was asserted that she received bribes from the Constable of Castille; this gave rise to the saying that 'Audley End was built with Spanish gold'. More seriously, however, the earl had appropriated public funds, and in 1619 was fined and imprisoned for embezzlement. The family's resources dwindled, the debts mounted and his descendants never recovered the great costs that he had incurred. In about 1668 James, the 3rd Earl, sold the estate to Charles II, reputedly for £50,000, and to enable the king to be close to the racing at Newmarket. Although the purchase price was never fully repaid, various monarchs used the estate successively until in 1680 Sir Christopher Wren identified the need for extensive repairs. The associated costs forced William III in 1701 to return the estate to the 5th Earl of Suffolk on condition that the remaining debts were cancelled.

In about 1721 the earl commissioned Sir John Vanbrugh (1664–1726), dramatist, soldier, herald and architect of Flemish descent. To reduce the upkeep expenses, Vanburgh advised the demolition of three sides of the western courtyard. When the Suffolk line died out in 1745, while Lord Effingham entered the estate without opposition, it was proved that the true heirs were the two daughters of James, 2nd Lord Griffin. Despite Lord Griffin's occupation the property was acquired by one of the daughters, the Countess of Portsmouth (d. 1762) in 1745 and it was she who in 1749 ordered that the long gallery of the eastern courtyard be demolished. The countess died without issue and left the property to her sister's son, Sir John Griffin (1719–97), field marshal, 4th Baron Howard of Walden and 1st Baron Braybrooke. He spent a further £10,000 and commissioned, in about 1763, Lancelot 'Capability' Brown and Robert Adam to design the gardens, which were 'not in order', a bridge, garden furniture, a suite of rooms and a Gothic-style

*The Tea House Bridge, Audley End House.*

chapel. The Temple of Concord was built by Thomas Furze Brettingham (1750–1806?), who had trained in Italy and was among other things a prison architect, to commemorate George III's recovery from a bout of madness in 1789.

Thus the mansion had become a shadow of its former self and formed the basis of the present stately home. The 3rd Lord Braybrooke, who inherited the house in 1825, and who tried to re-create its earlier state by destroying Adam's interiors (which were restored in the 1960s), is largely responsible for the present interior and furnishings which include works by Canaletto, Holbein, Kneller and Lely, a splendid doll's house and a collection of over 1,500 stuffed birds. After requisition during the Second World War the estate was returned to the 9th Lord Braybrooke, before being sold to the Ministry of Works in 1948 and thence to its present owners, English Heritage.

So the great house developed. In 1578 Queen Elizabeth I visited Audley End, received a deputation from Cambridge University, and was presented with a pair of perfumed and embroidered gloves. She, 'behoulding the beauty of the said gloves . . . held up one of hir hands; and then smelling unto them, put them half waie upon hir hands'. In 1664 John Evelyn described the house as 'one of the statliest palaces in the Kingdom . . . a mixt fabric, 'twixt antiq. and modern. . . . It shows without like a diadem, by the decorations of the cupolas, and other ornaments on the pavilions.' In 1669 Pepys tells of the housekeeper who 'took us into the cellar, where we drank most admirable drink, a health to the king. Here I played on my fflageolette, there being an excellent echo.' On his second visit he drank again 'of much good liquors. And indeed the cellars are fine; and here my wife and I did sing, to my great content. And then to the garden, and there did eat many grapes, and took some with us.' In 1697 Celia Fiennes noted that the mansion with '750 rooms . . . makes a noble appearance like a town, so many towers and buildings of stone within a park which is walled around' (quotations in Talbot and Whiteman). After Charles II acquired Audley End his queen, Catherine of Braganza, 'had a frolic to disguise themselves like country lasses in red petticoats, waistcoats &c., and so goe to see a fair' in about 1678. Probably at Saffron Walden they had overdone their disguises, and when the queen went to a booth to buy 'a pair of yellow stockings and long gloves stitched with blue', they were discovered and almost mobbed as far as the gatehouse.

While Samuel Pepys had played, sung and eaten at Audley End in the seventeenth century, music, singing and eating continue there today. World-famous classical orchestras and jazz musicians play almost on the site of the former smaller eastern courtyard during the summer to huge audiences which, with their picnics, stretch up the hill to the Temple of Concord. At the end of the concerts the great house forms a dramatic backdrop for the firework finale.

It is not surprising that a small hamlet should grow up near such a mansion and Audley End is no exception. Near the main entrance is a small number of Georgian houses which includes St Mark's College. Originally designed as almshouses founded by the Earl of Suffolk in about 1600 in a collegiate style with two courtyards of ten dwellings each, separated down the middle by a range consisting of a chapel, hall and kitchen, they became a home for the benefit of retired clergy.

Overlooking Audley End is the market town of Saffron Walden, 'a fair market-town which saffron may seem to have coloured the name thereof'. Early spelling, Wealh, implies a valley of Britons and it may be that the earliest settlement, known as Brookwalden up to the end of the sixteenth century, was down by the River Cam. Alternatively it may have been near Bridge End, known as Cheping or Chipping Walden throughout the Middle Ages. Saffron replaced Chipping at the end of the Middle Ages, when the autumn-flowering crocus, Crocus sativus (from western Asia, in Arabic sahafaran), was introduced. This was used up to the eighteenth century not only as flavouring and a medicine, but also as a yellow dye in the town's wool and cloth trade. In a groundless tradition, the crocus is said to have been brought to England in the fourteenth century hidden in a returning pilgrim's staff and introduced to Walden by Sir Thomas Smith (1513–77) in the sixteenth century. In all likelihood it was introduced to the region as early as the thirteenth century; certainly by the end of the sixteenth century it was well established.

Brookwalden was, arguably, the earliest inhabited settlement occupied by the Romano-British. It went on to play an important role both before and after the

Norman Conquest and the nearby abbey further enhanced its reputation. It owes its market to Queen Matilda and its corporation to Edward IV. Geoffrey de Mandeville founded its flint and rubble castle. Built between 1125 and 1141, it had a brief life as a castle, being made indefensible by Henry II in 1158. It remained habitable for about 100 years after and a round tower was added in 1796; now there are only a few remains. Here, according to Matthew Paris, in 1252 Roger de Leyburn (d. 1271), warden of the Cinque Ports, killed by chance 'a valiant knight Ernauld de Mounteney'. The castle did not long survive de Mandeville's downfall and it soon became derelict.

The town was built upon a medieval grid where 'a narrow tongue of land shoots itself out like a promontory, encompassed with a valley in the form of a horseshoe, enclosed by distant and delightful hills. On the bottom of this tongue are seen the ruins of the castle; on the top, the church. The houses are ranged on the side of the hill and in the valley around the church, the base of which, being as high as the buildings, is discerned above the roofs' (William Stukeley to Roger Gale, c. 1710). The description holds today, and on the grid are many largely seventeenth-, eighteenth- and nineteenth-century houses, at least one of which, the Sun Inn, dates in part from the fourteenth century. Although no longer an inn, it was used by General Fairfax in 1646 as his headquarters. Its celebrated and amazing pargeting dates from around this time; two giants support the sun, one wielding a club, the other a sword. According to some they represent Gog and Magog; according to others they represent Tom Hickathrift fighting the Wisbech giant for the right to use a forbidden road. Tom won.

St Mary's Church is among the finest and largest churches in Essex. Dating from the fifteenth century, and the third church on the site, its design is attributed in part to Simon Clerk and John Wastell. It is more a splendid building than a spiritual one, being some 200ft long with a spire 193½ft high. Inside the church is a remarkable black Tourrai marble monument to Thomas Audley. It is described by Fuller (in Murray) as a 'lamentable epitaph' of the Lord Chancellor, founder of *M-AUDLEY-N* College, Cambridge, and also by Fuller (in Jenkins) in 1662 that the marble was 'not blacker than the soul, nor harder than the heart, of the man whose bones lie beneath it'.

> The stroke of Deathe's inevitable dart
> Hath now, alas! of lyfe beraft the hart
> Of Syr Thomas Audley, of the Garter Knight,
> Late Chancellour of Englend under owr Prince of might
> Henry Theight, wyrthy high renowne,
> And made him Lord Audley of this town.

First recorded around this time, although its exact date of origin is probably much earlier, is Saffron Walden's curious antique maze. Surrounded by an earth bank and cut into the turf, and possibly a copy of a much earlier maze, it consists of a series of fourteen concentric brick circles surrounding a central mound. Four spokes radiate from this mound. They cause pairs of circles to be turned back upon themselves but allow the next circle to pass through. Three outer paths form four 'bastions'. To 'tread the maze' and reach a girl at the centre involves a walk or run of about half a mile.

In addition to Sir Thomas Audley and Henry Winstanley, Saffron Walden's sons include Roger Walden (d. 1406), possibly a butcher's son who went on to become secretary to Richard II, Lord High Treasurer, Archbishop of Canterbury and Bishop of London; Thomas Walden or Netter (d. 1430), a Carmelite monk who became Confessor to both Henry V and Henry VI, dying at Rouen; the Protestant martyr John Bradford (1510?–55), once chaplain to Edward VI and who dedicated his last letter, 'a Dying Martyr's Testament to the Faithful at Saffron Walden'; Sir Thomas Smith (1513–77), provost of Eton, Secretary of State and Queen Elizabeth's ambassador to Spain, and a friend of his, Gabriel Harvey (*c.* 1550–1630) who dabbled in astrology and gained a degree of immortalisation through his friend Edmund Spenser who not only dedicated the introduction of *The Shepherd's Calendar* to 'the most excellent and learned both Orator and Poete, Mayster Gabriell Harvey', but also wrote him into that work as Hobbinol (quotation in Crouch).

Between 1929 and 1965 R.A. (Rab) Butler (1902–82) was the Conservative MP for Saffron Walden. In 1965 he became master of Trinity College, Cambridge, and the life peer Baron Butler of Saffron Walden.

*The River Cam at Littlebury.*

Growing in stature, the River Cam continues south past the Ring Hill Iron Age fort. Underneath this fort is the first railway tunnel from London, the southern portal of which bears the coat of arms of Lord Braybrook, while on top is Robert Adam's Ionic temple commemorating the end of the Seven Years' War. The fort's inhabitants may have moved north to what is now the sizeable village of Littlebury (a fortified Saxon settlement). Its prosperity belongs first to the early sixteenth-century wool trade and secondly to the early nineteenth-century coaching days. Noteworthy houses include the sixteenth-century Gatehouse Farm, the Granta House and, with its mansard roof, Mill House, built in about 1700. The village became the home of Henry Winstanley (1644–1703). Initially he was Clerk of Works to Charles II at Audley End. He went on to design the first Eddystone lighthouse and while supervising its construction was captured by the French, who then destroyed that which had been built. After his release he completed the works which were again destroyed, this time by a great storm in November 1703 which claimed not only his life but also those of his five companions.

In Little Chesterford, about a mile north of Littlebury, is one of the oldest inhabited houses in Essex. The Manor House, with stone walls about 3ft thick dates from the thirteenth century and has early fourteenth- and fifteenth-century additions.

*The River Cam at Little Chesterford.*

The church also dates from the thirteenth century and contains a memorial to James Walsingham (1646–1728). He was the last of the principal line of the Walsingham family that is believed to have taken its name from Walsingham in Norfolk. Erected by his sister, the work is signed by Henry Cheere (1703–81), who made statues in marble, bronze or lead for gardens and for funeral monuments. He was knighted in 1760 and created a baronet in 1766.

The last riverside village in this part of the county is Great Chesterford. This village probably migrated south to its present position from an early Palaeolithic settlement and a later Roman fort which had been built to guard a river crossing. As such, the fort would have attracted a considerable Saxon civilian population which would have settled outside the Roman walls, thus establishing the present village. The large restored church dates from the thirteenth century. A stone tablet outside the south door bears the slightly unfair inscription: 'How dreadful is this place' (Genesis). A short distance below Great Chesterford weir, the River Cam, the M11 and the railway line almost merge to cross the county boundary from Essex into Cambridgeshire.

# 2

# Into Cambridgeshire

The first Cambridgeshire village the small river encounters is Ickelton, according to Camden 'an ancient little city' where the Icknield Way crossed the Cam. It was 'The town or homestead of the Icen . . . the first inhabited place within the borders of the Iceni which was reached by the traveller in his progress eastward along the Ickneild [*sic*] Street' (quotation in Murray). Its early Saxon/Norman church of St Mary Magdalene is unique. The massive circular pillars forming the arcade are Roman monoliths of Barnack stone originally from Northamptonshire. Three explanations of their presence are put forward. Some say they were moved from the ruined Roman building lying just to the south discovered in 1847 while others suggest they were moved from the Roman station at Great Chesterford. However, bearing in mind their size, a more feasible explanation is that the pillars were never moved and that they were in fact the remains of a Roman villa around which the Saxons subsequently built their church. If this is so, and it seems a likely explanation, then they form a unique in situ example of Roman architecture.

In August 1979 an arsonist stacked books and vestments around the organ and set fire to them. While it took two years to repair the church at a cost of some £280,000, there was a plus. An almost complete small set of twelfth-century wall paintings was discovered.

About 650yd to the west of the church, Abbey Farm marks the site of a priory of Benedictine nuns dedicated to St Mary Magdalene founded in the late twelfth century by Aubrey de Vere, 1st Earl of Oxford. This priory was not the only one to possess land in the parish. Abbeys at East Dereham (Norfolk), Tyltey (Essex) and Calder (Northumberland) each possessed a manor. While Henry VIII gave them all to Thomas Goodrich (d. 1554), Bishop of Ely, in exchange for the more valuable Hatfield House, Elizabeth I demanded that they be given back as a condition of appointing Martin Heaton (1552–1609) as bishop of that see. Having reacquired the manors, the Crown then sold them; financially, the Crown did well.

The river, still very small, separates Ickleton from Hinxton. Its church of St Mary and St John, having some Norman work, not only contains a brass of Sir Thomas de Skelton (d. 1416), steward to John of Gaunt, portrayed in full armour and accompanied by his two wives dressed in long gowns with draped headdresses, but also a rare parochial register. Dating from about 1538, it is one of the first such documents.

*Between Ickleton and Hinxton.*

Hinxton has come a very long way since the Saxon Hengest had his 'tun' or farm. The red-brick late seventeenth-century Hinxton Hall and its estate became a science centre, initially owned by Tube Investments Ltd where major metallurgical research was undertaken. In 1992 the Wellcome Trust bought the estate and now its startling modern buildings form the Sanger Centre where the internationally respected research into genome sequencing takes place.

Across the river again to the east is Duxford, formerly Duxworth. Named after a local chief Ducca, whose enclosure it was, it consisted of at least four separate hamlets. Two neighbouring hamlets grew rapidly during the twelfth and thirteenth centuries. They each had their own church, St Peter in the south and St John in the north. Both have Norman origins, but that of St John, built on the site of a temple of the Templars and later the Hospitallers, has been disused since 1939. According to Arthur Mee its spire, on its central tower, became bent not through old age but through the pulling up of a flagstaff for Queen Victoria's Diamond Jubilee in 1897.

Duxford Mill dates from the Norman era and is mentioned in the Domesday Book. It was burnt down, rebuilt in the fifteenth century and modified in the sixteenth. Its old wooden wheel, 18ft in diameter and over 8ft wide, was replaced with an iron wheel in the 1890s. Visited during the Civil War by Oliver Cromwell and in the nineteenth century by Charles Kingsley, it may have given the latter inspiration for *The Water Babies*, some of which was written at the mill when he stayed there in the 1890s.

*The River Cam at the site of Duxford Mill.*

Like Hinxton, Duxford has its share of research facilities. Duxford developed specific smells as the traditional corn-grinding industry turned initially to bone grinding and then to coprolite grinding for fertiliser. This led to the establishment of the Cambridge Fertiliser Company, which was taken over by the agricultural giant Fisons.

In 1934 Dr de Bruyne, who had worked on synthetic resin adhesives, founded Aero Research in Duxford. During the Second World War not only was wood glue used for the manufacture of gliders and Mosquito fighter-bombers, but also a metal to metal adhesive was developed for use in aircraft and tank clutches. The facility became a part of the Ciba Geigy Plastics Division, synthetic resins and glue, and in turn the company Novartis. The site, Huntsman, now houses various research facilities including Cambridge Biopolymers.

For there to be a research facility at Duxford associated with aircraft is not surprising. On the site where in June 1647 Oliver Cromwell's army assembled in defiance of an order from Parliament to disband, an airfield was built. Taking two years to build, it was opened on 1 April 1918 and used initially for training, among others, trainee American airmen. In 1920 the airfield became home for a short time to 2 Flying Training School before its removal to Digby in Lincolnshire, after which RAF Duxford's role gradually became that of a fighter station. Among the first units to be stationed there were 19, 29 and 111 Squadrons. Its huge neo-

Georgian-style barracks were completed in 1933, and two years later, on 6 July, King George V, with over 100,000 spectators, reviewed his Royal Air Force.

At the outbreak of the Second World War Duxford, a sector control airfield, was home to 19, 66 and 611 Squadrons equipped with Spitfires. It was also home to 222 Squadron. Initially equipped with Bristol Blenheim aircraft that were replaced with Spitfires in March 1940, the squadron was commanded by the then Flight Lieutenant Douglas Bader, who was later to command the famous Duxford Wing with its five RAF fighter squadrons. Other squadrons based at Duxford included 312 (Czech) Squadron, 302 (Polish) Squadron, both equipped with Hurricane aircraft, and 74 Signals Wing. By 1943 all the British operational units had been removed elsewhere. The airfield was handed over to the United States Eighth Air Force and it became the home of the 78th Fighter Group equipped initially with P-47 Thunderbolts and subsequently with P-51 Mustangs. The group was credited with destroying some 1,400 enemy aircraft by the end of the war.

After the war Duxford was handed back to the RAF and it remained an operational airfield with Gloster Meteor jets, Hawker Hunters and Gloster Javelin delta-wing fighters replacing the Spitfires, Hurricanes and Mustangs. By the early 1960s, however, it became apparent that its facilities were insufficient to cater for a new breed of jet fighters such as the BAC Lightning. The last operational flight was on 31 July 1961 by a Meteor T7. Except for a short period when the airfield was used by the film industry for such films as *The Battle of Britain*, the airfield remained essentially unused. While possible future uses included a prison, an industrial storage area and a sports centre, it was an approach by the Imperial War Museum that was to secure the airfield's future. A new site had been found to house the museum's extensive collection of historic aircraft. The first aircraft, a P-51D Mustang and a Hawker Siddeley Sea Vixen, arrived in spring 1972. In 1976 it was opened on a daily basis to the public. In 1997 the American Air Museum, in a glass-walled hangar designed by Sir Norman Foster, was opened.

Today the airfield is home to First World War aircraft such as the British RE 8 with a top speed of 102mph and the American Spad S.VII biplane. Second World War aircraft include the British de Havilland Mosquito, Supermarine Spitfire, Westland Lysander, Avro Lancaster and Short Sunderland flying boat; the German Messerschmitt Me163B-1a Komet and Junkers Ju 52/3m, possibly of Portuguese abstraction; and the American B-25 Mitchell, Boeing B-17 Flying Fortress 'Sally B' and a Boeing B-29 Superfortress 'Hawg Wild'. Postwar military aircraft include those from Britain, France, Canada, Sweden, Argentina and America. As befits a war museum, exhibits at the museum are not confined to aircraft: there are tanks, artillery and midget submarines.

In addition to military aircraft, the airfield is home to civilian aircraft, including an ex-Dan-Air Comet, an ex-Cambrian Airways Viscount, an ex-Monarch Airlines Britannia, an ex-BOAC/British Airways VC-10, an ex-BEA Trident Two and, arguably in pride of place, the Anglo-French BAC/Aérospatiale Concorde 101. From its first flight in December 1971, it was only used for test purposes and it held the record for the fastest Atlantic crossing by a civilian airliner: 2 hours 56 minutes.

It arrived at Duxford on 20 August 1977, piloted by Brian Trubshaw, Concorde's British chief test pilot.

By way of direct contrast about a mile to the west in a direct line with Duxford's runway and lying between Duxford, Pampisford, Sawston and Whittlesford, or, as they are called in a local rhyme, Dirty Duxer, Silly Panser, Proud Sawston and Long Whitser, is the thirteenth-century chapel of the Hospital of St John. The small chapel, only chancel and nave, was mentioned in 1286 as having being established *ab antiquo tempore*. It had a small endowment of some 60 acres of meadowland and a water mill equivalent to some £200 per year. Duxford chapel, sometimes known as Whittlesford Priory despite being in Duxford parish, was under the direction of a prior appointed by the Bishop of Ely. It is now maintained by English Heritage. Part of the fabric of the hospital, perhaps used as a hostel up to the Reformation, is believed to be incorporated, appropriately, into the nearby much-restored seventeenth-century Red Lion Inn.

In the stonework of the tower of Whittlesford's Church of St Andrew is carved a small Sheila-na-gig consisting of a human-headed male animal and a naked lady. Inside the church is a small chapel dedicated to St John the Baptist. It was in his

*The Chapel of the Hospital of St John.*

honour that a small guild raised money for the church and its guildhall, a much-restored early Tudor house that remains in the centre of the village. The Baptist Ebenezer Hollick, known as 'young' Ebenezer, who died aged eighty-seven in 1828, built the mill house in 1763. Four years later some forty Baptists were 'dipped' in the mill pool.

Despite its name Pampisford was not connected with a ford; its early name was Pampesworth, the enclosure of Pampa. It lies close to a much damaged length of the Brent Ditch. This was one of many such ditches in East Anglia probably built in the seventh century when the Kingdom of Mercia was at odds with the Kingdom of East Anglia, to assist movement along the Icknield Way between the higher chalk uplands and the lower fens. The ditch runs close to Pampisford Hall. Its owners, the Parker Hammond family, enlarged the original 1830s house in French and Italian Renaissance style in the 1870s. Robert Marnock (1800–89), who had among other things worked near Florence, designed its formal gardens. In the park, well known in Victorian times, is a remarkable collection of fir trees from Japan, Mexico, China, California, Australia and the Pyrenees.

Pampisford Mill, mentioned in Domesday, was converted from a grain mill to a paper mill in 1802, and in 1893 the Eastern Counties Leather Company purchased it. In 1926 it was taken over by an employee, Charles Moore, whose descendants still run the business four generations later.

Sawston, formerly Salsingtune, adjoins Pampisford to the north. In the centre of the village is Sawston Hall. It was acquired in the early sixteenth century by the Huddleston Family, which had long been established in Cumberland, through William Huddleston and his marriage with one of the co-heiresses of the Marquess Montague. Remaining in the Huddleston family until the 1960s, it is the only surviving Elizabethan courtyard house in the county built of clunch and not brick. Mary Tudor was the instigator. In 1553 on the death of her brother, Edward VI, Protestant lords, led by the Duke of Northumberland, sought to arrest her as she approached London. She took refuge in Sawston Hall with William's son, John Huddleston, quoted by Mee as 'once Chamberlayn unto Kinge Phylipe and Captaine of his Garde, and one of Queen Maryes most honourable Privie Counsil'. Her presence was reported to Cambridge and a Protestant mob under direction pounced on the hall so quickly that she barely had time to escape to Framlingham, according to tradition on horseback dressed as a dairymaid behind Sir John or a servant. Angry at her escape the mob set fire to the house, virtually all of which was destroyed.

As an expression of her gratitude Mary Tudor promised to have the house completely rebuilt using clunch from the recently destroyed Cambridge Castle. In the inner courtyard two dates, 1557 and 1584, together with the initials of two Huddlestons, could mark the beginning and end of construction. Towards the end of the rebuilding a more thoroughgoing Protestant persecution had broken out. To hear Mass was treason and the officiating priest invariably suffered a lingering death. At Sawston the chapel was built into a garret together with secret hiding places and secret exits. The priest's hiding hole at Sawston was described by Allan Fea and quoted in Coneybeare:

The entrance is so cleverly arranged that it slants into the masonry of a circular tower, without showing the least perceptible sign, from the exterior, of a space capable of holding a baby, far less a man. A particular board in the landing is raised, and beneath it, in a corner of the cavity, is found a stone slab containing a circular aperture, something after the manner of our modern urban receptacles for coal. From this hole a tunnel slopes downwards, at an angle, into the adjacent wall, where there is an apartment some twelve feet in depth, and wide enough to contain half a dozen people. . . . The opening is so massive and firm that, unless pointed out, the particular floor board could never be detected, and when secured from inside could defy a battering ram.

According to Coneybeare the Priest's Hole was built by the Jesuit Nicolas Owen (d. 1606), nicknamed Little John because of his diminutive stature. 'With incomparable skill and inexhaustible industry . . . many priests were preserved from the prey of the prosecutors.' Sadly for him he was betrayed to the Protestant government. 'Knowing his skill in constructing hiding-places, and the innumerable number of these dark holes which he hath schemed for hiding priests throughout the kingdom' it was hoped that he would reveal all. Despite being tortured, ultimately to death, he kept the secrets. The governor of the Tower reported, 'The man is dead – he died in our hands.'

Nearly 300 years later, in 1820, there were other fires, some twenty-three, in and around Sawston. They appeared to be caused by spontaneous combustion, as they would unexpectedly burst into flames despite the presence of guards. The local fire brigade responded quickly, limiting the damage. However, one day the captain of the brigade was noticed standing close to a haystack with a ball of smouldering peat. He had discovered that if he pushed it deep into the stack, fire would suddenly break out hours later, a trick which he may have learnt from those who set light to fenland fields. Each time he was called out to extinguish the fire he was paid 5s. For conducting this little business he was duly executed.

The leather and tanning industry has been long established in Sawston and a letter dated 7 October 1804 written by Jane Huddleston to her brother Richard Huddleston describes a strange short-lived incident which occurred in the tanner Thomas Adams's house. Over a period of five or six days virtually everyone in the house, men and women, had their clothes torn in 'a manner [they] could not account for'. It was 'impossible to describe how much some of the cloaths are torn, quite strong cotton gowns, so that no beggar would accept them. . . . It cannot be done by any liquid drops for the cloaths are evidently rent, tho' no one hears them rend.' One visitor thought she had escaped; however, when she stood up she 'opened the part of her gown that had been under her arms the whole time, when to her astonishment she found it rent in four places'. At the end of the week 'many persons from Cambridge, as well as from neighbouring villages, visited the house and returned without injury to their cloaths' (quotation in Porter). Porter wonders if Mrs Adams's fifteen-year-old niece had anything to do with the incident.

As well as the tanning industry, which expanded to include chamois leather, and passed through the ownership of Eastern Counties Leather Company to Craftsmen Chamois Ltd, Sawston was for centuries a centre for paper manufacture. In 1836 Edward Towgood bought Sawston Paper Mill, formerly known as Borough Mill, from the widow of Charles Martindale who is believed to have installed at the mill one of the first paper-making machines in Britain. Edward Towgood converted the mill to steam power and it became well known for producing fine grades of paper, particularly for ledgers and parchment. Spicers Stationery Manufacturers have occupied the site since 1915.

Besides Sawston Hall, Sawston, the mill of which at Dernford was first recorded in a charter of about 954, contains some ancient houses. Brook House is believed to date from the thirteenth century and the Queen's Head from the fifteenth. A sixteenth-century custom lasted until recently. In 1554 the imprisonment of a widow for stealing peas may have been John Huntingdon's inspiration for a bequest made in his will that every year 2 acres of his land should be sown with peas for the relief of the poor.

*The River Cam near Whittlesford.*

Across the still small river again, to the west, is Whittlesford, which at Domesday consisted of the main village which is centred on an early abandoned medieval moated site and an outlying hamlet. But for a disagreement, Whittlesford Mill would have become, under a proposal by Sir Hamilton Kerr (1903–74), MP for Cambridge, the country home of the leader of the opposition (as Chequers is for the prime minister).

Both parts were occupied during the Roman occupation and a story is told (in Porter) of the discovery of some Roman remains including some skeletons. A labourer, Mathews, took a skull and put it on his mantelshelf. The following night a loud knocking on his door awoke him. Looking out he saw a headless skeleton in the garden below. A deep hoarse voice asked for its head to be returned. Terrified, Mathews threw it out at once to its true owner.

The River Cam flows north through Dernford Mill, now the site of a strategic gauging station belonging to the Environment Agency, to join after half a mile the River Granta on the outskirts of, to the east, Great Shelford and its urban sprawl towards Cambridge, and to the west, Little Shelford.

On a hillock overlooking Little Shelford is the Wale Obelisk, a stone pillar on a pyramidal base commemorating 'Gregory Wale Esq., Justice of the Peace for the County. Deputy Lieutenant. County Treasurer. Conservator of the River Cam. . . . A Good Subject, an Agreeable Companion. A Faithful Friend, a Hospitable Neighbour. And in all parts of Life a useful Member of Society. He died June 5th 1739 in the 71st year of his age. Universally lamented and was buried in the Parish of Little Shelford. This Obelisk was erected by his surviving Friend James Church Esq., as a Public Testimony of his regard to the memory of the noble gentleman.' His grandson was General Sir Charles Wale (1763–1845) who served in Gibraltar and the West Indies. 'In February 1818, at the head of his brigade the Royal York Rangers, he decided the capture of the island of Guadeloupe from the French' (quotation in Scarfe). A colonel of the 33rd Duke of Wellington's Regiment of Foot, who received his knighthood in 1815, Wale became a general in 1838 and died at Little Shelford. His son, Frederick, was killed in action at Lucknow.

> Folks in Shelford and those parts
> Have twisted lips and twisted hearts.

Great Shelford, Scelford, a shallow ford, developed like Whittlesford from two small Saxon manors, both identified at Domesday, one close to the ford through the River Cam and the other about half a mile away across a meadow on a small stream. A medieval bridge, once in the charge of a hermit, replaced the ford. Gradually the two settlements merged to form, by the fifteenth century, a triangular village that remained essentially unchanged until the late nineteenth century. Centred around the railway station, the first on the railway line south of Cambridge, there was rapid development followed by a further sprawl along the road all the way into Cambridge.

Across the river again to Hauxton, Havochestum, the mill bridge of which was paid for by the grant of forty days' indulgence to all who aided the project. Near this

*The River Cam between Little Shelford and Great Shelford.*

mill and prehistoric ford, possibly where the Mare Way crossed the river, a mass cemetery or, as described by some, a bone yard, was discovered in 1875. There was a large quantity of human and horse bones, mixed with swords, shield bosses, daggers and small bronze plates inscribed with runes, dating from about 870. Of particular interest was a round green glass brooch engraved with the snake-headed raven of the god Woden.

Hauxton's little Norman church of St Edmund, standing on the site of an earlier wooden church, contains on the east wall of the south aisle a very rare half-length fresco of St Thomas Becket. The site of Thomas's murder in Canterbury became a place of pilgrimage for many and a good source of revenue for the Church. Henry VIII detested the Thomas cult. At the dissolution Thomas's festivals were suppressed, effigies destroyed and his name erased from service books. This painting, showing Thomas with a cross in one hand and the other raised in blessing and dating from about 1250, was saved from both Henry VIII and Thomas Cromwell by being bricked up and plastered over. It was forgotten until 1860 when it was accidentally discovered during restoration work.

The mill, also mentioned in Domesday, was used in the late eighteenth century for crushing rape seed for oil. Following a fire, the mill was rebuilt in 1851 and continued working until 1974, incorporated, with Hauxton Hall, into Fisons Agricultural Division.

About half a mile below Hauxton the River Cam or Rhee joins the river and it flows, now called the River Cam, or locally the River Granta, towards Cambridge.

# 3

# The River Granta

As with the Bourn Brook, a railway line ran along the River Granta valley from Cambridge and Stapleford almost to its headwaters at Bartlow. Here it divided, one branch turning north-east out of the catchment towards Haverhill and Colchester, and the other branch passing through Ashdon on its way to the main line to London at Audley End. Initially called the Colchester, Stour Valley, Sudbury & Halstead Railway, and incorporated into the Great Eastern Railway in 1862, the section from Cambridge to Haverhill was opened on 1 June 1865. When the line was being planned in 1863 it was proposed that it should pass between two of the four Bartlow tumuli. The committee of the Archaeological Institute intervened and a new route was chosen. Its intervention was too late to prevent some cuttings being made into the mounds where bones, possibly pre-Roman and which formed fifteen complete skeletons, were found. The line was finally closed on 6 March 1967.

The second branch, the Saffron Walden Railway, was opened through to Bartlow on 26 October 1866. While it was essentially intended for light traffic, express trains headed by heavy Britannia-class Pacifics passed along this route, which had to be specially strengthened for the purpose, during major engineering works in 1957 on the main London line at Great Chesterford. The line was closed to all traffic on 28 December 1964.

While there was a railway line running along the river valley, there was also one that crossed it at Bartlow. This was the Newmarket & Chesterford Railway, opened for passengers on 4 April 1848; it was built to provide a direct line from London to Newmarket, but did not prove popular. It was closed on 9 October 1851, since when trains to Newmarket ran via Cambridge, and finally abandoned in 1896.

Not only was Bartlow a railway junction but also it is at the junction of two branches of the upper reaches of the River Granta, which rise near Castle Camps in Cambridgeshire and near Ashdon in Essex, which branch is called the River Bourn (not to be confused with the Bourn Brook in the west of the catchment; see Chapter 6). The early Castle Camps, previously Great Camps, lies about half a mile south-west of the present village on a spur between two springheads of the river. Its name reflects one of the largest motte and bailey castles in the county, built soon after the Norman Conquest by Aubrey de Vere, 1st Earl of Oxford (d. 1141). The family, from Castle Hedingham in Essex, held it until 1580 as one of their hunting lodges at the centre of their south Cambridgeshire and north Essex estates. It is likely that the first castle was relatively small, since inside the main bailey are the remains of a smaller bailey which occupies only about a quarter of the area of the final castle. Another feature of this castle is that the present medieval church of All Saints stands inside the outer bailey on the line of the smaller inner bailey. Dating largely from the fifteenth century, but with some thirteenth-century fragments, the church is much newer than the castle and it is likely that the de Vere family built this church within the confines of their castle, possibly on the site of a much earlier church. The village, which had grown up around the outside of the castle and its church, was abandoned when the castle fell into disuse during the seventeenth century, probably after 1648 when the 20th Earl of Oxford had his lands confiscated by Parliament; the greater part fell in about 1738.

Over the hill in Essex the River Bourn rises near St Aylotts, a fifteenth-century house built on the site of an earlier building of the same name and owned by Waldon Abbey (now supplanted by Audley End House) in the thirteenth century.

*The River Bourn near its source at Ashdon.*

St Aylotts was the subject of the last letter of Thomas Howard, 4th Duke of Norfolk, to his son, the builder of Audley End, before he was beheaded for treason in 1572. Ashdon lies to the north of St Aylotts, and Waltons at Barrow End is a mid-eighteenth-century rebuilding for Sir William Maynard of an earlier Tudor house belonging to the Tyrell family. Sir John Tyrell (d. 1437) was MP for Essex and treasurer to Henry VI's household. His grandson, Sir James Tyrell, was the supposed murderer of the princes in the Tower. He was beheaded at the Tower in 1502 after confessing to the murders.

Ashdon is linked with Bartlow, and in particular Bartlow Hills, by an erroneous tradition. According to this tradition Bartlow Hills are the graves of heroes and 'all the flower of England', killed in action in the battle between King Cnut and King Edmund in 1016. However, the battle was actually in Essex 'at a hill called Ashingdon' in the River Crouch valley, not at Ashdon in the River Bourn catchment. The hills or mounds are indeed burial mounds, but they are Romano-British. Of the original seven, four are still recognisable, the largest being some 40ft high by 147ft in diameter. Excavated during the 1830s they were found to contain walled tombs. These held ornamental bronze ewers and other grave furniture including glass, enamel and earthenware bottles and lamps. They were all removed by the Maynard family to Easton Lodge near Dunmow which they had occupied since 1590. Sadly the finds did not see the light of day for long; in 1847 a fire at the lodge destroyed them all.

St Mary's Church is noteworthy for two reasons. First is its Norman round tower, one of only two such round towers in Cambridgeshire (the other being at Snailwell). The second is its fifteenth-century frescoes, which include one of St Michael weighing souls assisted by the Madonna and a demon, and St Christopher opposite the entrance of the church – and traces of a large dragon which is no longer accompanied by St George.

Between Bartlow and Linton the river flows past Barham Hall, which was constructed in about 1830. It was built on the site of a priory of Crutched Friars, which had been founded before 1292. Known variously as Crouched, Crutched or Crossed Friars they were one of several lesser orders that amalgamated in 1265 to form the Order of Austin Friars. Their principal house was at Little Welnetham near Bury St Edmunds in Suffolk and to which Barham Priory was attached. They had neighbours at Linton in the shape of another priory, which was attached to the Priory of St Jacutus de Insula in the diocese of Dule in Brittany. After the dissolution this latter cell was granted to Pembroke College in Cambridge. No traces of either site remain.

About half a mile to the south-west, overlooking the valley, is Hadstock with its late Saxon church of St Botolph. The iron-bound Saxon north door is claimed by Mee to be 'the oldest door in all England'. It is said to have once been covered with tanned skin, which upon investigation was proved to be human. It may have been the skin of a Dane killed during an attempt to plunder the church. Similar cases have been found at Copford (Essex) and Worcester. Whether legal or not, such a punishment was sometimes inflicted upon those who attempted to steal church property in the eleventh and twelfth centuries.

*The River Granta near Linton Mill.*

Linton, with its medieval houses, is more like a Suffolk wool town than a small Cambridgeshire village. It was a flourishing market town and its market granted in 1246 lasted until 1864. It was regarded as being of some importance since, like Caxton, it is one of the four places shown on Badesdale's map of Cambridgeshire of 1741 with a church symbol. Perhaps in this case that was indeed because of the thirteenth-century church of St Mary and its monuments. First is a brass portrait of a relative of Matthew Paris of Hidersham, Henry (Nicholas?) Paris dressed in armour and dated 1427. More striking, however, but hidden behind the organ, is a large marble monument to Sir John Millicent (d. 1577) and his family. Said to have been the Lord of Barham Manor, Sir John was a fanatical Protestant, a servant of Thomas Cromwell, who was nearly lynched for his beliefs during the Lincolnshire Rebellion of 1536. Indeed, he might not have been displeased to watch the severe rebuilding of the church in about 1870. He is depicted opposite his second wife, both reclining, holding her hand over a skull and hourglasses hanging by their sides. In a small compartment above them his first wife leans out and watches them, while in another small one below them are their eleven kneeling children.

According to a local legend, Linton did not escape the attentions of Dick Turpin (1706–39). Son of the innkeeper of the Crown Inn at Hempstead in Essex, just a few miles to the south-east, he joined another highwayman, Tom King, whom he had once thought to be an ordinary citizen and had even attempted to rob. Together they worked the Cambridge road until Tom was accidentally shot and killed by Dick, after which he, Dick, escaped to Yorkshire where he was eventually arrested for horse stealing and hanged at York. Before all this, however, the legend tells of an encounter between Dick and a wealthy local tanner, Thomas Mallyon (Maling). One winter evening, returning on horseback from selling hides in Cambridge, Thomas was joined by another rider. As they rode on together the stranger started to talk at length and in great detail about Dick Turpin's feats, so much so that Thomas suspected that the stranger was no other than Dick himself. Fearful that he was about to be attacked, Thomas tried to throw off his companion by galloping ahead. The stranger kept pace with him until Thomas, reaching the familiar fields near his home, drew ahead. He reached the safety of his house and his servants slammed the gates shut in the highwayman's face. The Old Manor House in Linton was never a manor house; it was formerly the tannery and home of Thomas Mallyon.

*The River Granta in Linton.*

*The River Granta at Little Abington.*

Linton seems an unlikely place to find an Indian eagle owl and a binturong, a long-haired fruit-eating Asian mammal. Housed at Linton Zoological Gardens, developed in 1976, they are believed to be the first to be bred and raised in captivity. The zoo, occupying some 16 acres and open to the public all year, takes part in the inter-zoo breeding programme for endangered species. Besides lion and tiger cubs, recent babies include a white-collared mongoose lemur and a western grey gentle lemur. It is believed the latter has only been successfully bred in two other places in Europe.

While Linton has one memorial to a member of the Paris family, it is likely that the family came from Carmarthen at the start of the fifteenth century to live in nearby Hildersham. Some say it might have been the birthplace of the thirteenth-century historian Matthew Paris (d. 1259); however, it was not his home for he entered St Albans Monastery in 1217. Sometimes known as the 'Father of English History', he continued writing the great *Chronica Majora*, which contained not only accounts of events in England but also in other countries, from 1235 until his death in 1259. In the medieval church of Holy Trinity are brass portraits of Robert Paris (d. *c.* 1408) and his wife Eleanor, Henry Paris (d. 1466), and another Henry Paris (d. 1472) and his wife Margaret. The proceeds from 'rubbing' these brasses brought in about £1,000 per year and helped to pay for much restoration in the 1970s. In contrast to these beautiful brasses is a gruesome skeleton of a Richard Howard who died in 1499. The Busteler family succeeded the Paris family in about 1630. The church used to contain two very rare oak figures of a cross-legged knight, said by some to be Sir Thomas Busteler, and supposedly the knight's wife with a dog at her feet. Sadly, these have been stolen and are believed to be in Belgium.

The Abingtons lie either side of the river, Little Abington on the north and Great Abington on the south bank. In the sixteenth century a pluralist, inappropriately named Thomas Goodman, held the two churches of St Mary. It was said 'He servethe not ye cure of Lyttle Abington in due tyme as he oughte to do and manye tymes uppon Satterdayes and hollye day evens he sayeth noe service at all, but ys aboute his owne busyness . . . more like a husbandsman than a minister' (quotation in Galloway). It is possible that there had been another church or chapel nearby. At Sunken Church Field, on Abington Church Farm, Porter tells of bells of a long-vanished church ringing underground and a ghostly choir singing under the grass.

Little Abington has another ghost, Jeremiah Lagden, a celebrated eighteenth-century highwayman of the Newmarket to London road. According to legend, he was captured on the Newmarket road and hanged in a field opposite his home, the Old House in Little Abington. A ghost of a highwayman haunts the spot and his name lives on in 'Jeremiah's Cottage'.

Babraham, formerly Badburgham, lies just beyond the clutches of the Cambridge suburbs. Philip Hardwick rebuilt its hall in Elizabethan style in 1832 for the Adeane family, the original Elizabethan parts having been demolished in 1767. In the latter part of the sixteenth century it was the home of the Genoese adventurer Sir Horatio Palavicino who was naturalised by patent in 1586. Among other things, he is said to have commanded a British ship against the Armada. He is also credited with developing early systems of irrigation for water meadows. From the dammed-up river he dug a 'leat' or ditch, from which water could flow through sluices over and across the meadow back to the river. In this way he was able to produce an early growth of grass for sheep.

By way of complete contrast, in Queen Mary's reign, he became the collector of papal dues, which he is alleged to have pocketed during Elizabeth's reign, and which may have enabled him to build the hall. These dues were known as Peter Pence; since the ninth century, the pope could claim by royal grant a penny a year for every house in England. Palavicino's epitaph (quotation in Coneybeare) recalls his work:

> 'Here lies Horatio Palavazene,
> Who robbed the Pope to lend the Queen.'
> 'He was a thiefe.' 'A thiefe? Thou liest;
> For why? He robbed but Antichrist.
> Him death with besom swept from Babram
> Into the bosom of Abram.
> But then came Hercules with his club,
> And struck him down to Beelzebub.'

Despite pocketing these dues he died 'an extreme miser' in 1600. Not to be outdone, his widow married Sir Oliver Cromwell of Hinchingbrooke, the Protector's great-uncle. Soon after, two of his sons married, on the same day, two of Sir Oliver's daughters. Perhaps this was not an uncommon event. In St Peter's Church an extraordinary black and white marble memorial by Jasper Latham depicts, in theatrical attitudes, Sir Richard (d. 1658) and Sir Thomas Bennet (d. 1667), two brothers, both baronets, who married two sisters.

Close by is a tablet to John Hullier, a Tudor curate who because of his faith became Cambridgeshire's only martyr when he was bound with chains, set in a pitch barrel and burnt to death. Books were thrown into the fire and 'By chance a Communion book fell between his hands, who received it joyfully, opened it and read so long till the force of the flame and smoke caused him that he could see no more. . . . His flesh being consumed, his bones stood upright even as if they had been alive, which the people afterwards took away, dividing them among them' (quotation in Galloway).

Babraham Hall is now a part of the Babraham Institute, an independent life sciences institute, with extensive futuristic-looking (in all senses) research facilities.

*Babraham Hall.*

Sponsored by the Biotechnology and Biological Sciences Research Council, with some 400 staff and an income of £16 million, it mainly carries out research into the mechanisms of cell and gene behaviour and how their failure or abnormality could lead to disease. Research into biomedical, biotechnological, pharmaceutical and healthcare projects is also carried out.

The parish of Stapleford, a suburbanised village of Cambridge, includes Wandlebury Hill Fort and the Gog Magog Hills, which although not exactly on the riverside are on the watershed and overlook the entire length of the River Cam. The circular hill fort, fancifully named by the thirteenth-century monk Gervase of Tilbury, is more than 900ft in diameter, and encompasses nearly 15 acres within two concentric banks and ditches. There were two principal building periods; the first was probably in the fifth and fourth centuries BC and the second, which included much repair work, during the late first century AD. There is widespread speculation as to its purpose. For example, Harper suggests it was the summer camp of a cohort of Vandals. This cohort was made up of barbarian prisoners defeated by Aurelian on the Danube, enrolled by Emperor Probus and brought over to terrify the British. On the other hand, in a logical but perhaps somewhat improbable account, Iman Wilkens, quoted by Cussler, argues that this fort and the Gog Magog Hills comprised the site of Troy and the Trojan War. In all likelihood, however, the Iceni built it as a defence against raiding tribesmen from northern France and Belgium, after which it would have been abandoned.

There is a very ancient legend told in 1211 by Gervaise in *Otia Imperia* (in Porter and Hawkes) that if a knight enters the fort during moonlight and shouts 'Knight to knight come forth' he will be faced with an armoured knight on horseback who charges until one of them is dismounted. A knight called Osbert who entered the fort alone and issued the challenge proved the legend. The armoured knight appeared and the two charged at each other, Osbert knocking his opponent to the ground. With misplaced confidence Osbert seized the other knight's magnificent, proud horse as his prize and started to lead it away. However, his rival had not yet finished with Osbert. In a final desperate effort he threw his lance at Osbert, wounding him in the thigh. Even though blood filled one of his boots, Osbert shrugged off the severe nature of the wound. In time it healed, but every year on the anniversary of the fight the wound opened afresh.

In the early eighteenth century the site was acquired by the Godolphin family and the entire inner rampart of the fort was demolished to make way for a new house, stables and landscaped gardens. It was the Godolphin family that planted the splendid beech woods which had the dual role of giving an elegant parkland setting as well as cover for game birds. Devotees of the Newmarket horse races, they owned one of the three original Arabian stallions that gave rise to many successful race-horse pedigrees: the famous Godolphin Arabian. Although the house no longer stands, the stables remain and the racehorse was buried under their cupola in 1753.

If the Gog Magog Hills, locally 'The Gogs', were in almost any other county than Cambridgeshire, they would hardly be distinguished as hills at all. The derivation of the name is obscure. Perhaps one of the earliest references to the names appears in

Ezekiel, 38–9: 'Son of man, set thy face against Gog, the land of Magog, the chief prince of Meshech and Tubal . . . and I will set fire on Magog and among them that dwell carelessly in the isles.' A singular mention appears in Revelation, 21, when the Devil had been released from his prison after a thousand years and had set out to deceive the nations 'which are in the four quarters of the earth, Gog and Magog, to gather them into battle'. Although the names are therefore of ancient origin, more recent theories include the suggestion that the names derive from 'Hog magog', a corruption of the High Dutch *hoog macht* (high power). Or perhaps the 'Hog' is derived from the Latin *hoga*, a height, and is related to the Hog's Back in Surrey. Michael Drayton (1563–1631) in *Poly-Olbion*, his poetical description of the topography of England, suggests a legend in which Gogmagog, a giant chieftain, fell in love with the nymph Granta. On his rejection he was transformed into a hill. Alternatively, it may relate to a prehistoric figure of a giant carved in the chalk, as instanced by John Laver, who in the early seventeenth century 'could never learn how these hills came to be called Gogmagog hills, unless it were from a high and mighty portraiture of a giant which the scholars of Cambridge cut upon the turf within the trench [the hill fort], but is now of late discontinued'. Such a figure was remembered in about 1724 and a graffito in St Mary's Church in Sawston of a pagan man brandishing a sword seems to corroborate this account. Whatever the exact origin, the ancient names appear to be an obvious play on words; a name with massive connotations applied to hills which rise to all of 230ft and which would be largely insignificant elsewhere.

As the River Granta flows on to join the River Cam at Great Shelford, it is sandwiched between housing and the track of the former railway line to Bartlow and beyond. Both the river and the old railway track seem, at least for the present, to have halted the southward march of suburban Cambridge.

# 4

# *The Upper River Rhee*

The River Rhee rises just over the Cambridgeshire border in the most northerly part of Hertfordshire. A small stream rises near Hinxworth Place, dating from 1460, once a cell of Cistercian monks from Pipewell in Northamptonshire, said to be haunted by the ghost of one of those monks, and described by Pevsner 'as one of the best preserved fifteenth-century stone manor houses of Hertfordshire'; but the Rhee's principal source, some 65 miles from the Wash, is in the village of Ashwell, or as it was known in the tenth century, Aescewellan.

According to Coneybeare, 'no prettier river-source is to be found throughout the length and breadth of England'. Its crystal-clear waters appear to bubble up in the middle of the village in a sort of amphitheatre, some 295ft by 82ft by 29½ft, with steep sides overshadowed by ash trees. These wide-spreading trees, favourites of William Cobbett, may not be the origin of the name but more the consequence; Axe was the Celtic for water. The water, once said to 'grip thirsty horse', maintains a more or less constant temperature of 11°C (52°F) and supports the rare Ashwell worms, *Crenobia Alpina* and *Polycelis Felina*, which are said to have lived there since the Ice Age. Their future has been ensured by strict controls on nearby water abstraction, which now render the 'spring' something of a sham. The water company maintains the flow at about 1 million gallons per day, some of which seems to flow into the amphitheatre from a pipe.

The spring is overlooked by the massive buttressed 177ft high tower of the fourteenth-century parish church of St Mary, crowned with a short narrow octagon carrying a characteristic feature of Hertfordshire churches, a small spire, or spiret, known as a Hertfordshire Spike. Thomas Everard releaded this spire in 1714 and on the roof recorded his work:

> Tho. Everard
> Laid me here
> He said to last
> An Hundred year.

While the spire, albeit somewhat twisted, is particularly fine, Thomas Everard may have taken his cue from St Mary's principal claim to fame: its remarkable collection of mainly fourteenth-century Latin/Greek graffiti inside the tower. Among these are the words of an apparently frustrated medieval architect who wrote 'The corners are

*Ashwell Springs.*

not pointed correctly: I spit at them.' Possibly it was the same architect who carved low down on the north wall a picture of the old St Paul's in London, with its rose window but with its 508ft-high spire rather than its dome, perhaps as an example of what could be achieved.

A four-line graffito deals with the aftermath of the Black Death. Locally the worst phase was in 1349, when it was estimated from diocesan records that up to 85 per cent of the population died. By 1350, while the worst was over, those that survived lived a miserable existence. The plague itself lingered on until a great storm on 15 January 1361 was supposed to have cleared the air of the infection. A translation of these four lines reads:

> 1350. Miserable, wild, distracted, 1350.
> The dregs of the people alone survive to witness.
> And in the end a wind
> Full mighty. This year St Maur thunders the world. 1361.*

---

* 15 January was St Maur's day. He was a sixth-century saint, the first to introduce monasticism to France.

Despite many instances of new developments, owing no doubt to the relatively easy access to London, the village is particularly English and arguably belongs more to Cambridgeshire than to Hertfordshire. The Black Death apart, it was a prosperous small market town and many of its fine medieval timber-framed and plaster buildings have survived despite a fire in the eighteenth century. In Mill Street a former maltings was converted into a small Merchant Taylors' school by the London livery company in 1681 and later used as a further education centre. The school requires restoration and its grounds have been 'developed'. Other noteworthy buildings include the fourteenth-century Bear House, St John's Guild House founded in 1496, a small gabled sixteenth-century Town Hall in Swan Street and presently a little museum, the sixteenth-century Rose and Crown, the Three Tuns, the Bushel and Strike near the church, and the manor house of Ashwell Bury remodelled by Luytens in the 1920s.

The young River Rhee flows north out of Ashwell and shortly after joining the Hinxworth tributary becomes the Cambridgeshire and Hertfordshire county boundary. At Mob's Hole near Guilden Morden it is joined from the south-east by another tributary which rises to the east of Ashwell. The county boundary turns back along this later tributary and so the two streams enclose the small, most northerly part of Hertfordshire. For the next half a mile as far as Hooks Mill, the site of a water mill and neighbouring tower windmill, the Rhee forms the boundary between the old county of Huntingdonshire and Cambridgeshire.

To the south-east of the mill is Guilden Morden from whence in 1845 twenty-three villagers set out for America. On 4 August their ship, the *Cataraqui*, was

*Morden Hall.*

wrecked with the loss of all the villagers. Unaccountably, at the exact time of the wreck St Mary's Church bells tolled. This church, which had belonged to Barnwell Abbey in Cambridge, with its massive Northamptonshire stone tower and needle spire, is one of the biggest in the county, reminiscent of the great Suffolk wool churches. Mainly fourteenth century but with some thirteenth-century remains, it was not the first church in Guilden Morden; in the fourteenth century an oratory in the grounds of the original manor house served the parish. Of particular interest is the rare and beautiful early fourteenth-century rood screen on which are depicted Bishop Erkenwald, brother of St Etheldreda who founded her abbey at Ely, and King Edmund of East Anglia holding, symbolically, the arrows by which he was martyred by the Danes in 870. The large mass cemetery, with its Iron Age and Romano-British origins, is noteworthy. A large collection of funerary relics has been found, including one male and two female decapitated bodies, indicative perhaps of earlier witchcraft practices.

Parts of the present Morden Hall may date back to the late fourteenth century. After the Peasants' Revolt, when Thomas Hasledon's original manor house was destroyed, he rebuilt his house on a new site within an imposing moat. The hall now remains among the best-preserved moated houses in the county with its lands home to a large herd of alpaca.

The Rhee now flows north-east in a relatively wide valley past the partly moated Tadlow Bridge Farm, the original site of an early manor house. First held by Sheriff Picot, the manor was subsequently granted to Fulk Fitwarine III (d. 1256), a baron who, opposed to King John, was excommunicated before making his peace with Henry III. In the seventeenth century this manor together with the rest of Tadlow, including the manor of Hobledod (thirteenth and fourteenth centuries), the manor house of which was just to the east of the thirteenth-century church of St Giles, was acquired by Sir George Downing.

Sir George (1685–1749) was the third baronet who held land in Cambridgeshire, Bedfordshire and Suffolk. He was born in East Hartly in west Cambridgeshire and inherited his grandfather's considerable fortune. At the age of fifteen he was married to his cousin Mary then aged only thirteen. Because of their youth and because Mary became a maid of honour to Queen Anne in 1703 they never lived together. In 1717 he obtained an Act of Parliament that sanctioned this arrangement, although they were not actually divorced. By his will, also of 1717, he left his East Anglian estates in trust for certain relations for the eventual founding of a Cambridge college carrying his name. While his heir died in 1764, Lady Downing was still alive and she refused to give up the estates. After some thirty years of litigation Downing College, with a considerably reduced fortune, was finally founded by charter in 1800 and the lands were held until their release in 1947.

As the Rhee flows in a more easterly direction, it passes yet more moated sites in the tiny settlements of Shingay and Wendy (an island on a river bend), or, as they are collectively known, Shingay cum Wendy. While Shingay now has no more than a few houses, it was once of considerable importance. It was here in the extensive moated site beside Manor Farm that, in the 1150s, the manor house became one of the earliest preceptories of the Knights Hospitallers of St John of Jerusalem. Although the establishment was small, a preceptor, two knights and three priests, one of which acted as vicar at Wendy, appear to have been skilled farmers, to such an extent that together with its estates in Wendy, Croyden and Arrington it became the fourth wealthiest in England and Wales. In the middle of the fourteenth century the Knights Hospitallers owned about 100 acres which yielded a gross income of £187 12s 8d of which 38 per cent was raised from the land. Their expenses amounted to about one-half of the income. At its dissolution in 1540 they owned property in forty-two parishes in Cambridgeshire and Cambridge and the establishment was handed over by Henry VIII to his Master of Hawks, Sir Richard Longe, who converted it into his country house. It was eventually demolished in the eighteenth century.

The Knights Hospitallers had a peculiar source of income which arose because their house had been exempted from every ban. Under an edict during King John's reign no religious rites could be observed. This included the burial of the dead to such an extent that 'you might see human bodies lying everywhere about the fields unsepultured'. At Shingay, however, the consolations of religion were freely available; Mass continued and the dead could be buried, so those who could not be buried in their own churchyard were spirited away to Shingay in a 'fairy cart' (feretorium, a bier on wheels). The practice continued for years and it included the burial of suicides and criminals. Indeed in about 1640 John Layer of Shepreth recorded that people executed in Cambridge were buried in Shingay. Of all this nothing now remains following a massive reduction in the size of the village.

The land between Shingay and Wendy seems open, uninteresting and relatively uninhabited save for cattle and horses. This dates back to the Middle Ages when cattle were quite rare and consequently the pasture became known as 'The Dairies'. The land was also subjected in the mid- to late nineteenth century to one of Cambridgeshire's oldest and unique industries that stretched from Soham on the edge of the Fens to Barrington nearby, namely the digging of coprolite, phosphatised clay nodules used as a fertiliser. Trenches were dug and the land yielded about 740 tons of nodules per 2½ acres. This method of extraction had some strange consequences, in particular gushing artesian springs which were reported to reach a height of 6½ft to 10ft. In Wendy, by the lane leading to Guilden Morden, a digger humorously placed an old gatepost over one such spring so that the water gushed picturesquely out of the top.

Between Shingay and Wendy the Cheney Water or Mill River, which rises just over the hill from Guilden Morden at Steeple Morden, joins the Rhee. 'Steeple Morden's silly people sold their bells to buy a steeple', and the tale goes on to say that the six bells were hung in Guilden Morden church. The steeple of the thirteenth-century St Peter and St Paul appears to have fallen down at least twice, first in 1633, flattening the chancel, and second during a great storm in 1703; the present small steeple looks strangely out of proportion to the main church.

Another tale is told (in Porter) of two murders and a ghost. In the mid-eighteenth century a packman was staying at Moco Farm during one of his regular visits. One morning he did not appear, indeed he was never seen again. Was it coincidence that the well at the farmhouse was never used again and filled in? Soon after his disappearance the farmer overheard his maidservant, Elizabeth Pateman, boasting to her fellow that she had a secret to tell him. The farmer and his wife assumed that Elizabeth knew what had befallen the packman and so, to keep her quiet, they murdered her. She was just nineteen and was buried in the churchyard of Steeple Morden on 21 February 1734. On her tomb were depicted a pea hook, a knife and a coulter, the implements with which she had been murdered. In the early twentieth century a couple staying in a cottage that had once been a part of Moco Farm were, for several nights, disturbed by the sound of a girl crying out as if in pain. On investigation they discovered that Elizabeth had returned to the spot where she had been murdered.

Cheney Water derives its name from the manor at its headwaters, which between 1015 and 1136 had belonged to Winchester Cathedral and was held in the fourteenth and fifteenth centuries by the de Cheyneys. It flows north-east to Abington Pigotts where there are three moated sites, each a former manor house. At Domesday the settlement was called Abingtona, Abba's farm. The Bishop of Winchester owned the pre-Norman Conquest estate of Abingdon Manor and it was eventually ceded to the family of Pigott (Pyot, Pygot). While the last of that line was killed in Flanders in 1794, the name was carried on by the Foster Piggotts until 1899 and of course by the village itself. In the fourteenth century the Pigotts left their original site, which was possibly in an area called the Rookery, and built another manor house in a moated site, previously the manor house of another pre-Conquest estate, the manor of Feugere, to the north of the church. In the mid-fifteenth century the family made their money from enclosing and converting arable land to pasture for sheep and thus wool. John Pigott, described as a woolman in 1461, became one of East Anglia's leading wool merchants. A third pre-Norman Conquest manor was the manor of Down Hall to the south-west on Cheney Water. While the present hall is nineteenth century, it has a beautiful, apparently fifteenth-century, small timber-framed gatehouse sitting astride the moat. It may be even earlier as carbon dating has placed some of the timbers as being between 1250 and 1380. The bell-capped lantern was a much more recent addition primarily for the benefit of travellers.

So the Rhee, gaining in size, flows east under Ermine Street at Arrington Bridge. This was an important posting station and river crossing and when the new bridge was built Roman artefacts and the bed of a gravel ford were found. The earliest bridge appeared during the thirteenth century. The road was becoming increasingly important; however, its upkeep, usually carried out parish by parish, was extremely poor and totally inadequate. The exception was the bridge, which was described by John Layer in the early seventeenth century as being 'maintained at the charge of the county and is one of the greatest passages now in the Kingdom'. It was, though, not always reliable and still the road had on occasions to be forded. In 1662 'travellers and their horses passing that way in the time of the great frost and high waters are forced to go through the river to their great danger' (quotations in A. Taylor). It was thus the overall state of the road that led to the setting up in 1663 of the first

*Down Hall, Abington Pigotts.*

turnpike trust in the county, under which tolls could be collected from travellers and then used for maintenance.

Just below Arrington Bridge the River Rhee intersects one of the finest works of the early eighteenth-century royal gardener Sir Charles Bridgeman (1680–1738): a magnificent 2-mile-long tree-lined avenue that runs from the southern edge of Wimpole Hall Park to a large octagonal pond fed by the river and on to Ermine Street. The park developed under the guidance of distinguished landscape gardeners such as Bridgeman, Capability Brown (1716–83), Sanderson Miller (1717–80), 'the gentleman provider of ruins' (quotation in Pevsner), Humphry Repton (1752–1819) and William Shenstone (1714–63) who, although poor at land drainage, loved water:

> Yon stream that wanders down the dale,
> The spiral wood, the winding vale,
> The path which wrought with hidden skill,
> Slow twining scales the distant hill

> With fir invested – all combine
> To recommend the waving line.

By the early eighteenth century the park was said to be 'worth riding twenty miles out of the way to see' (quotation in Scarfe), and had subsumed over 200 years the ancient village of Wimpole. In the early seventeenth century it was a flourishing village with a post mill standing on a mound, itself probably the site of a twelfth-century castle motte, a church, roads and houses with gardens. Many of them can still be traced through the prominent earthworks in the park, which exactly match the detail shown in a contemporary map of 1638. Even Sanderson Miller's Gothic folly, built on the northern edge of the park and aligned exactly with the southern avenue, is not such an unlikely feature of an earlier time.

Surrounded by 600 acres or so of some of the finest parkland in the country, Wimpole Hall, with its formal gardens, is one of the finest country houses in Cambridgeshire. Building of the original house started in about 1632 and was completed in the 1650s for Sir Thomas Chicheley (1618–99). Sir Thomas, High Sheriff of Cambridgeshire, Master-General of the Ordnance and MP successively for Cambridgeshire and Cambridge, lived an extravagant lifestyle and in 1686 was forced to sell the estate. It was bought by the Earl of Radnor who remained there for fourteen years before selling it to the Duke of Newcastle.

*Wimpole Hall.*

Within a year the duke died and the estate passed to his sole heir, Henrietta, who three years later married Edward Harley, 2nd Earl of Oxford (1689–1741), in the hall's drawing room. Not only did he spend much on the hall and its grounds, but he added to his father's collection of books and manuscripts. Sadly, he became an alcoholic and in order to pay off his debts he was forced to sell the estate for £100,000 to Philip Yorke, the 1st Earl of Hardwicke. The hall's contents were sold in 1742, the 'Harleian Library' being bought by the bookseller Thomas Osborne and the British Museum.

The estate remained with the Earls of Hardwicke until about 1888, during which time they represented Cambridgeshire as Members of Parliament from 1780 with only a short break between 1810 and 1832. In 1843, Admiral Sir Charles Yorke, the 4th Earl, entertained the young Queen Victoria and it is said that, through some muddle, the attendant in charge of her jewels was not forthcoming. Not to be outdone she came down with a wreath of roses in her hair. Someone commented that 'not all the jewels in the world could make her look more Queenly' (quotation in Coneybeare).

The Hardwickes' reign came to an end with the 5th Earl, 'Champagne Charlie' and companion to the Prince of Wales, who had inherited the estate in 1873. Within fifteen years he had accumulated debts of £300,000 and like his predecessors at Wimpole, Chicheley and Harley he was forced to sell the estate, which was subsequently acquired by Lord Robartes. Its last private owners, Captain George Bambridge and his wife Elsie, the daughter of author and poet Rudyard Kipling, acquired the hall in 1938. After George's death in 1943 Elsie remained, living as a recluse but passionately devoted to the house, until her death in 1976, after which the estate, including the late eighteenth-century Wimpole Home Farm and now a home for rare breeds, was handed over to the National Trust, so the public can now visit this great hall and park. But it was not always thus. Elsie, who had become very possessive of the hall, when she saw people picnicking in the grounds, would get their car registration number. She would trace them to their home whereupon she would later turn up in her chauffeur-driven car and in turn picnic on their lawn!

A small stream flows around the northern edge of the park and before it joins the River Rhee at Malton Farm flows through Orwell. In the mid-nineteenth century it was described as being very pretty, with a spring flowing out of the hillside, known as Toot Hill (old English for Look-out Hill), into a well shaded by magnificent trees in the middle of a prehistoric earthwork close to the church. In 1870 it was found that the earthwork contained coprolite worth about £100. For this small sum all was destroyed. Orwell's church of St Andrew, mainly thirteenth century but with some Norman fragments, has been added to over the centuries. One particular addition is the chancel, built by the then rector as a memorial to Sir Simon Burley, lord of the manor. Sir Simon (1336–88) had been a soldier and a courtier; he was a companion to the Black Prince and became tutor and guardian to one of his sons, Richard II. Unfortunately, because of his pupil's failure to learn how to govern, Sir Simon was impeached and beheaded in 1388.

On the south side of the valley lie Melbourn and Meldreth, divided by and linked to the River Rhee by the River Mel. From its Neolithic origins, through its bestowal by King Eadgar to the monks of Ely, Melbourn became an important village in the Middle Ages, with several moated houses and a medieval church.

In the late 1630s there was countrywide resentment against the fiscal policy of Charles I; no less in Melbourn. In 1640 under the village trysting-tree the villagers resisted his taxes, particularly one called 'ship money'.

And they fell upon the sheriff's men with stones and staves and hedgestakes and forks, and beat them and wounded divers of them, and did drive them out of the highway into a woman's yard for their safety. And were forced for saving their lives to get out of the town a back way; which, notwithstanding some thirty or forty able men or boys pursued them above a quarter of a mile, stoning them, and driving the bailiffs into a ditch, where some of their horses stuck fast. And the multitude got some of the bailiff's horses and carried them away, and would not redeem them without money (quotation in Coneybeare).

*The River Rhee at Malton.*

The village's prominence waned during the nineteenth century and in 1850 it was reported that all but 30 out of 200 houses contained more than one family and indeed one was said to house thirteen families. By the twentieth century it had become an important centre for fruit growing, particularly greengages; during the season an average of 30 tons per day were sent by train to London from Meldreth station.

Separated from Melbourn by the River Mel, the Cambridge to London railway line and the A10 trunk road is Meldreth, where a Bronze Age hoard of axes, spears and swords has been discovered. Once again it must have been of some early importance, since its Norman church, situated close to the river and some distance from the present centre of the village, was one of only three churches in Cambridgeshire, outside Cambridge, mentioned in Domesday. It was here that the preacher Andrew Marvell the Elder (1586?–1641) and father of the poet and satirist Andrew Marvell the Younger (1621–78) was born. By this time the village had evidently declined in importance; while Melbourn is shown on mid-seventeenth- and early eighteenth-century maps, Meldreth is not. It is likely that the present village had migrated towards the railway line built by the Great Northern Railway in 1851.

The River Mel also joins the River Rhee at Malton. Although it is now a very tiny place, there are remains of extensive moats and traces of a church. It is likely that, situated strategically on the river, it was of some earlier importance as it is shown as a village having a church on both Robert Morden's (1669–1703) and Richard Blome's (1660–1705) seventeenth-century maps of Cambridgeshire, but spelt as Walton.

# 5

# The Lower River Rhee

Below Malton the River Rhee valley becomes wide and flat, particularly to the south and east. Between Malton and Barrington two tributaries join the river. Their sources lie some 7½ miles to the south on the chalk uplands near the watershed settlements and villages of Newsells, Barley, Great Chishill and Heydon.

Newsells, with its neo-Georgian-style house which replaces a Queen Anne house, carelessly burnt down during the Second World War, lies midway between Barkway and Barley in Hertfordshire. Although Barkway is situated outside the River Rhee catchment, it is at the end of a unique series of milestones which start at Great St Mary's Church in Cambridge. They line an old coaching route which ran parallel to the River Rhee through Trumpington, Newton, Fowlmere and Barley to Barkway and beyond to London. Between 1586 and 1599 the Master of Trinity Hall College in Cambridge, William Mouse, and his friend Robert Hare jointly left £1,000 in trust to the college, with the interest to be applied to mending the road for 16 miles between Cambridge and Barkway, in *et circa villam nostram Cantabrigiê prêcipue versus Barkway.*

Apart from Roman milestones, there were few other milestones in England and it was not until the Turnpike Act of 1698 that the Turnpike Trusts were required not only to maintain the roads but also 'to measure them and set up a stone every mile' (quotation in Harper). On 20 October 1725 the then Master of Trinity Hall, William Warren, set up the first of a series of stones; five more were put up during the following year and a further five the year after that. The final, sixteenth, stone was erected on 29 May 1728. Among the earliest milestones the fifth, tenth and fifteenth were massive stones about 6½ft high engraved with the black crescent of Trinity Hall. The intervening small stones, noting miles only, were replaced with larger stones between 1728 and 1732, all now bearing the black crescent.

Barley was to become home to a remarkable collection of intelligentsia, all but one connected in some way with the Church. William Warham (1450?–1532) had been rector between 1495 and 1501, and went on to become Archbishop of Canterbury in 1504. While he crowned Henry VIII and Catherine of Aragon, he was later approached by Cardinal Wolsey who suggested that their marriage was null and void. In 1630 King Henry forced him to advise Pope Clement VIII accordingly and that he, William, would be a competent judge to determine their divorce.

A hundred years later Andrew Willett (1562–1621) was the rector between 1599 and 1621. Chaplain and tutor to Prince Henry, he was the father of Thomas Willett

(1605–74), who having joined the second Puritan exodus to Leiden and then New Plymouth, became the first mayor of New York in 1665 and 1667. Yet another rector, Thomas Herring (1693–1757), went on to become not only chaplain to George I and the Archbishop of York but, like his predecessor, Archbishop of Canterbury from 1747 until his death.

Although Redcliffe Salaman (1874–1955), a former doctor and an expert in the genetics of potatoes, was not directly connected with the Church, his friend James William Parks (1896–1981) was a world authority on Jewish–Christian relationships. Having narrowly escaped assassination by the Swiss Nazis, he established a research centre in Barley between 1935 and 1964 for the study of Jewish–Christian relationships.

Barley had had an earlier link with Germany; in its churchyard is buried one of conservative Germany's greatest aristocrats, Heinrich, Count Arnim (1814–83). He disregarded the call to arms of his own country and joined in the struggle for Hungarian liberty. Not only did his vast estate thus become liable to forfeiture, but also he risked spending the rest of his life in a military prison. The personal and bitter animosity of Bismark, and the hatred of two powerful families and relatives of two opponents he had killed in duels aggravated these dangers. To avoid prison, he fled to England, assumed the name of Loeffler with the rank of major, set up a school for fencing and physical exercise, and married a German governess.

His association with Barley arose from his friendship with the rector who attended his school and in whom he had confided his real identity. On behalf of the count's son, the rector wrote to the German Emperor and as a result the son was allowed to

*The Fox and Hounds at Barley.*

join the German army and enjoy his father's estates. Unfortunately for him, his mother, who according to German society was neither of noble birth nor ennobled through marriage, accompanied him. Consequently, while he moved in the highest social circles, she was restricted to the servants' hall. The count recalled them to England, saying 'I would rather have my son grow up a poor man in England, in the service of his adopted country, than as a rich man in the service of his Fatherland, where he would have had to be ashamed of his mother' (quotation in Harper). Because of his friendship with the rector, he chose Barley as the final resting place for himself and his wife, being buried at midnight by torchlight in accordance with old German customs.

The road east out of Barley towards Great Chishill passes under a replica gallows inn sign depicting a procession of fox, hounds and huntsmen. The original, said to have been placed in allusion to a fox that took refuge in a dog-kennel of the inn, was destroyed when the old Fox and Hounds inn was burnt down in 1950. Before reaching Great Chishill the road passes, on the top of a spur, a beautifully restored small post mill. It was built in 1819 with materials from an earlier mill which had been constructed in 1726. Unlike some post mills it has a 'fan-tail' as opposed to a 'tail pole', for turning the mill to the wind. Although now in Cambridgeshire, it was not always so; before 1895 both Great Chishill and Little Chishill lay in Essex. In 1798 a great fire wiped out nearly all of Great Chishill, only sparing its church, dating from the early fourteenth century with some fifteenth-century graffiti and dedicated to St Swithin, an entirely appropriate dedication for such a dry area on a watershed.

Heydon, whose lord of the manor once held a curious service for his tenure, namely the requirement to hold a towel for the monarch during the coronation service (probably last performed during the coronation of George IV), cannot claim to be at the headwaters of the River Rhee. It was, however, directly connected to one tributary by the Heydon or Bran Ditch. Although this ditch has since been ploughed flat, it ran for about 3½ miles from the high woodland at Heydon, north across the Icknield Way to the former mere at Fowlmere. Probably built as a defensive ditch by the Saxons or Romano-Britains during the mid- to late fifth century, it consisted of, on the west side, a deep ditch filled with brush, next to a steep grassy slope leading to a rampart or vallum. It hindered east to west movement along, particularly, the Icknield Way and was probably linked with the bitter fighting associated with the mid-fifth-century Saxon revolt, the early sixth-century re-establishment of Roman rule and the seventh-century dispute between the Mercians and East Angles. Groups of skeletons have been found, some with war-wounded soldiers and another with the remains of at least fifty-six men, women, and children who must have perished during a savage massacre. Nearby a chamber cut into the chalk was discovered in 1848, containing a crude altar and a large number of Roman artefacts; its use is not clear.

Not only does the Bran Ditch cross the Icknield Way, but also it crosses the Rhee's tributaries near Flint Cross. The Icknield Way was one of Britain's major prehistoric routes, running from near Brancaster on the north Norfolk coast, in a southerly

*Great Chishill Windmill.*

direction across Norfolk, Suffolk and Cambridgeshire, then south-west below the northern edge of the Chilterns, across the River Thames and on towards Salisbury. It was not metalled like the roads built by the Romans, but more a track or series of parallel tracks which led across a narrow belt of country where there was neither fen nor forest to hinder travel. Under the laws of William I the Icknield Way was one of four roads which were granted privileges. Any traveller slaying or assaulting another on one of the roads would be held to have committed a breach of the king's peace.

The principal river tributary continues northwards, passing Flint Cross, so named after the former remote Flint Inn, to Fowlmere. Fugelesmare at Domesday, it took its name from the nearby marshy lake or mere, overgrown with reeds and populated with wildfowl. Although Sir John Rennie drained the mere in the mid-nineteenth century, the land remained full of springs and rivulets. It was the perfect ground for waterfowl and is now the site of the present nature reserve and visitor centre run by the Royal Society for the Protection of Birds. Its waters form the first of the two tributaries joining the River Rhee below Malton.

Lying on or close to coaching routes, Fowlmere's three inns, the Chequers, the Swan and the Black Horse, prospered. In February 1660 Samuel Pepys left London by horse at 7 a.m., hoping to reach Cambridge by nightfall. After 46½ miles he reached Fowlmere, his 'mare almost tired', and spent the night at the Chequers. Whether it was the present Chequers is debatable; a stone on the inn is inscribed with the initials W.T. and the date 1675, said to refer to one William Thrift who improved the inn at that time. Either the inn was quite new when Pepys arrived, since half the village was destroyed in a fire of 1634, or it had suffered and needed restoration. Whatever the case Pepys continued his journey the next day, reaching

*The Chequers at Fowlmere.*

Cambridge at 8 a.m. The Church of St Mary, standing on the site of a Norman church, although much restored in 1869, has some thirteenth-century remnants. It is noteworthy that between 1561 and 1925 there were only eleven rectors, one of whom, John Crackanthorpe, served for an amazing fifty-three years. Passing Fowlmere, the tributary, now more of a brook, flows between Shepreth to the west and Foxton to the east.

The historian John Layer (*c.* 1586–1641) noted that Shepreth was 'environed on all sides except the south-east with rivers and brooks and has a pleasant sweet brook besides running through the middle of the town'. In complete contrast, in about 1900 Shepreth was described by Harper as

> this soddened village . . . not a place of great or polite resort, for the lane is a narrow twisting way, half muddy ruts and half loose stones. Beside it crawls imperceptibly in its deep ditch-like bed, overhung by pollard willows, a stream that takes its rise in the bogs of Fowlmere. . . . Here and there old mud-walled cottages, brilliantly white-washed and heavily thatched, dot the way; the sum total of the village, saving indeed the church, standing adjoining a farmyard churned into a sea of mud.

He gives a general impression of damp and decay.

Others dispute this view and echo Layer's description, painting an entirely different picture. According to Coneybeare (*c.* 1910), Shepreth is 'a little gem of a village with a clear and copious brook running across its maze of thick-shaded lanes'. Mee (*c.* 1953) describes it as 'charming . . . with lovely groves of trees and murmuring brooks and thatched cottages dotted about the lanes'. According to Cook (*c.* 1953) it was 'as pastoral as its charming name . . . following the curve of a willowy stream. Little bridges, flower filled gardens of old-fashioned dwellings, geese wander idly over the road'. These latter descriptions pertain more today.

Although Shepreth and Foxton virtually run into each other, each has its own railway station. In about 1848 the Great Northern Railway attempted to reach Cambridge from London and so break the Great Eastern Railway's monopoly. A line was opened up but, in the interests of the Great Eastern Railway, Parliament would not allow the Great Northern to proceed beyond Shepreth. So Shepreth, a 'nowhere place', became the final halt of the Great Northern's venture. However, its passengers were able to continue to Cambridge; no one was able to prevent them being conveyed by a Great Northern coach. This practice, involving a forty-minute journey, continued for four years after which the Great Eastern not only built a line from its main line at Great Shelford, through Foxton to Shepreth, but also gave running powers to the Great Northern right through to Cambridge.

The railway companies had their effect on local architecture. County stations built by the Great Northern, such as at Shepreth, tended to consist of a two-storey block projecting on to the platform. On the ground floor were the station offices and on the upper floor the stationmaster's rooms. This arrangement afforded a good view up and down the line. In contrast, while some of the large Great Eastern stations were Italianate, such as at Cambridge or Ely, smaller ones were built around a square block with a low-pitched slate roof, with the stationmaster's house at the rear, such as at Great Shelford and Foxton.

The Fowlmere Brook joins the River Rhee which here formed part of the boundary between Mercia and East Anglia. Now dominated by vast quarries cut back into the white chalk hill to the north which, together with their supporting infrastructure, produce cement, Barrington has long been associated with mineral extraction. Initially this was because of the presence of the upper greensand, rich with organic remains and where 'coprolites' were discovered in the late nineteenth century. These were not true coprolites, but rather nodules rich with lime phosphate. They were worth some £3 per ton with an average yield of some 300 tons per acre. At the height of the industry 55,000 tons a year were extracted. Merchants were willing to pay at least £150 per acre for three years' digging and were obliged to reinstate the land when digging finished. Washings from the nodules were used for landfill and making bricks. The nodules themselves were ground to powder at Royston and sulphuric acid was added to produce super-rich phosphate of lime fertiliser.

The greensand also yielded copious quantities of mainly Pleistocene fossils, many of which are in the Geological Museum in Cambridge. They include the remains of mammals from a semi-tropical climate such as bears, lions, elephants and hippopotami. It was said that a good 'fossil digger' could earn £3 per week. Not only have flint implements and cut red-deer antlers been found, indicating human presence here at least 5,000 years ago, but Neolithic, Roman and Anglo-Saxon remains have also been discovered.

Barrington was to become the home of one of the oldest English country families, namely the Bendyshe family. While the family had held land there, its principal estate had been at Radwinter. That estate, however, had been mortgaged in order to raise money for Edward III during the siege of Calais. Unfortunately for the Bendyshes, the monks to whom the property had been mortgaged foreclosed the deal before the money could be paid back, so the family was forced to move to their lands at Barrington. In recognition, Edward III granted a market every Wednesday and a fair to be held on St Margaret's Day (later moved to Ascensiontide).

At about the same date as the Bendyshe family moved into the hall, in 1324 Hervey de Stanton, chancellor to Edward II, founded and conferred property to Michaelhouse College in Cambridge. While it was subsequently incorporated into Trinity College, it could be claimed that, because its statutes pre-date those of Peterhouse College by some fourteen years, Michaelhouse was the earliest embodiment of a Cambridge college. Trinity College, and not the Bendyshe family, became patron of the living and indeed clunch from the pits was used in building that college. Other materials were used in the construction of the Gate of Honour at Gonville and Caius and in the First Court of St John's College in Cambridge.

Mineral extraction was not the only industry at Barrington. In the late 1940s Peter Ward of Grantchester spent his spare time making and repairing singing birds, which led to him becoming a scientific instrument maker. Initially he worked alone at the bottom of the Old Vicarage garden in Grantchester in a Gothic folly given to his father by Rupert Brooke's mother, and made laboratory water baths. He moved to the old water mill at Barrington and the company familiar to laboratory workers worldwide was created, namely Grant Instruments, its name recalling the early days in Grantchester.

Between Barrington and Harston another tributary, which rises to the south-east near Duxford (see chapter 2) and flows through Newton, joins the Rhee. A Saxon

*The River Rhee at Harston Mill.*

village, Newton was first recorded in a will of 976 when it was given to King Edgar. Much of the village was burnt down in a fire during the summer of 1746 when, reputedly, apples hanging on the trees were roasted. Two wings of Newton Hall survive from this date. In 1909 a neo-Queen Anne front was added by Sir Charles Waldstein (later the 1st Lord Walston and second director of the Fitzwilliam Museum in Cambridge), giving the building its massive appearance. In 1967 the National Seed Development Organisation, which was concerned with patenting and licensing plant breeding techniques, was established at the hall.

On the watershed between the Rivers Rhee and Cam, on Maggot's (Margaret's) Mount, a slender obelisk marks the spot where in the mid-eighteenth century two friends, one from Newton and the other from Little Shelford, met every day for years. When one, Gregory Wale, died in 1739, the other, Charles Bottomley, erected a memorial in his friend's memory: 'He lived an advocate to liberty.' Rowley's Hill, overlooking the River Rhee, was the site of a late eighteenth-century semaphore telegraph station, one of a line in use between London and Cambridge. Harston lies below this hill.

Now very much an urban and industrial sprawl that has become established along the A10 trunk road, the old village with its church of All Saints lies close to the river. It marked the end of the Mare Way, a prehistoric ridgeway and one of the oldest identified tracks in Cambridgeshire which ran from Kingston near the Bourn Brook along the watershed through Orwell and Haslingfield to the old ford at Harston. This became one of the most important river crossings in the county and there have been water mills here since the thirteenth century. The church's roof is supported by a strange series of carved figures all with large heads. They include a man eating a loaf, another crouches on a pot while an odd thin man holds his ears, a nearby monk makes a face and an old man sits sadly with his head on his knees. The pulpit is one of the few medieval wooden pulpits in the country.

Haslingfield lies on the east side of the river. Built around its church and ancient hall, the nearby fifteenth-century chapel, Our Lady of White Hill, with its image of the Virgin Mary, was at the centre of Easter pilgrimages until the Reformation. While there are no remains of the chapel, in 1885 a lead bulla of Pope Martin V (1417–31) bearing the faces of St Peter and St Paul was found. It was to this chapel that Thomas de Scales (1399?–1460) dedicated his chains in thanksgiving for his release after he and his colleagues, Sir John Fastolf (1378?–1459) and John Talbot, 1st Earl of Shrewsbury (1388?–1459), had been comprehensively defeated in about 1429 near Patay by Joan of Arc. That he did this was not surprising since the Scales family had held the manor since the mid-thirteenth century.

The Wendy family acquired the manor in 1541, and it was the first Sir Thomas Wendy who built the early large Haslingfield Hall with wings and turrets. Now only a shadow of its former self, as late as 1814 the building was still complete, surrounded by gardens and a moat. Soon afterwards, the house was reduced and its chimney removed to Bourn Hall. Thomas (1500?–60), who had studied medicine at Ferrara, was physician to Henry VIII (and attended his deathbed), Mary I, Elizabeth I and Edward IV. He was also a friend of Dr John Caius (1510–73), who had

*The River Rhee at Haslingfield.*

studied medicine in Italy at Padua, not very far from Ferrara. It was he who re-founded Gonville College in 1565, 'a miserable little institution . . . in a deplorable state' (quotation in Steegman), as Gonville and Caius, Thomas Wendy being the major benefactor.

The Norman Church of All Saints, given in about 1250 to St Mary's Abbey in York, contains many documents to the Wendy family, some in contemporary dress. A window not only contains a pane with a coat of arms of the Scales family, but also a memorial to Bishop Charles Frederick Mackenzie (1825–62), once vicar of Haslingfield and who, perhaps coincidentally, had been educated at Gonville and

Caius. As Bishop of Central Africa, consecrated bishop in 1861, he is shown preaching to natives in Africa against a background of chained slaves marching through the jungle. He went to Africa in 1854 and working with Dr Livingstone he freed many slaves. One time on his way to meet Livingstone his canoe was overturned on the River Ruo. He lost his quinine and after a short stay on the Island of Malo, caught fever and died. He was buried in Malawi, close to the confluence of the River Ruo and the River Shire, a tributary of the Zambezi, opposite Malo, on the edge of a forest among the natives. It is said that Livingstone himself marked his grave with a cross (quoted in Mee).

From the top of Chapel Hill it was claimed that, in one of the widest panoramic views in England, it was possible to see the River Cam valley past Cambridge to Ely and Swaffham Prior to the north and east and, to the south-west, Sharpenhoe near Dunstable; a span of about 50 miles and containing eighty churches (quoted in Coneybeare and Mee). It overlooks an ancient river crossing, at Burnt Mill Bridges, to Hauxton on the prehistoric route from Bourn to Great Shelford. While no trace of this crossing remains today, the river here could have been the inspiration for some lines in Milton's 'Il Penseroso':

> There, in close covert, by some brook,
> Where no profaner eye may look,
> Hide me day's garish eye,
> While the bee with honeyed thigh,
> That her flowery work doth sing,
> And the waters murmering,
> With such consort as they keep
> Entice the dewy feathered sleep.

Passing Cantelupe Farm, the River Rhee joins the River Cam or Granta that started its journey 18½ miles to the south near Amberden and Henham in Essex.

# 6

# *The Bourn Brook*

The Bourn Brook rises just to the east of Eltisley near Caxton End, where a generally flat area known as the western clay plateau has replaced the chalk. Thick forests became established and as the first settlers moved in they started to clear the woodland. Their Saxon successors completed the task, and by the eleventh century the landscape became fully developed, with the Bourn Brook cutting its way through the plateau to join the River Cam at Byron's Pool. Settlements became established along the valley and elsewhere in the sporadic clearances.

Not only was there a river in the valley but there was also a Roman route, the Lot Way, which ran essentially along this valley from Cambridge via Grantchester, Barton, Comberton, Toft, Caldecote, Bourn, Caxton and Eltisley towards St Neots. In some cases villages, such as Caxton, lie directly on the line of this route, in others, such as Caldecote, while the settlement may be a short distance away, the church lies on it.

So in the valley there was a river and an ancient road, and there was also a railway. The railway was part of the Cambridge to Potton Railway, which in turn formed part of the Bedford and Cambridge Railway and the cross-country Cambridge to Oxford Railway. Under an Act of 1860 it was opened on 1 August 1862 and incorporated into the London North Western Railway in 1865. Closed in 1966/7, it followed the valley from Byron's Pool to Bourn, with a passenger station at Lord's Bridge near Barton and amenities for goods at Toft and Kingston. After Bourn it turned south-west towards Sandy and Bedford. Part of the track bed to the south of Barton is currently used for Cambridge University's Mullard Radio Astronomy Observatory. Its telescopes, like huge mobile ears, give the landscape a somewhat surreal appearance.

Eltisley, Hecteslei at the time of Domesday, lies on the boulder clay on the watershed of the westward-flowing Abbotsley Brook and the eastward-flowing Bourn Brook. It had, according to a sixteenth-century tradition, a convent of Benedictine nuns as early as the ninth century. It was to this convent, where her cousin was the prioress, that Pandionia (Pandiana, Pandonia or Pandrionia), the daughter of a Scottish king, fled to preserve her honour. She remained there until she died in about 904, by which time she might well have become the prioress. She was first buried near a well, to whose waters healing powers were attributed. This well could have been in the hummocky ground just outside the south wall of the

*The Church of St Pandionia and St John, Eltisley.*

church. In about 1344 her body was removed into the Church of St Pandionia and St John. St Wendreda was her companion.

While one tradition says that William the Conqueror destroyed the ancient nunnery at Eltisley and the nuns went to Hinchingbrooke near Huntingdon, another tradition says that the Benedictine nunnery at Hinchingbrooke was actually founded by William in 1087. Whichever is true there seems little doubt that there had been an ancient nunnery in or around Eltisley. Where it was is not exactly known. It could be that the essentially thirteenth-century Church of St Pandionia and St John was built on its site. Perhaps the hummocky ground is further confirmation and of course the priory would have had a well. Indeed, the early English antiquary John Leland (1506?–52) refers to an 'old priory . . . over the hedge to the south of the church'. On the other hand, in the thirteenth century the Bishop of Ely confirmed the existence of a ruined chapel about a mile to the north at Papley Grove and whose lands were ceded to Denny Abbey near Waterbeach.

As for the well, the reputed healing powers of its waters became so well known that by the 1570s it had become a place of pilgrimage. The rector, Robert Palmer, had his own views about this. He considered it was a 'site of idolatrous and popish practices' and consequently he broke it down. By all accounts he was an unusual man, since he decapitated some thirteenth-century effigies in the church, and was accused of taking paving slabs from the church for his own use, of allowing the vicarage to be used as an ale-house and of playing cards during church services (Eltisley Millennium Committee).

During the summer of 1234 a dramatic storm occurred. It was described by the monk and chronicler of St Albans, Roger de Wendover (d. 1236). In his account the storm was widespread, as he relates it not only to Eltisley but also to 'Alboldesley', presumably Abbotsley some 3½ miles to the south-west.

According to Roger, during a severe famine the starving poor invaded the fields of the ripening harvest and devoured the crops,

> for which they may scarce be blamed. Of the farmers, however (who ever from their avarice, look upon the poor with an evil eye), many were highly wroth at this pious theft. And they of Alboldesley hied them all on the next Sunday (the sixteenth of July) to the church, and with tumult required the priest to excommunicate on the spot all who had thus plucked their wheat-ears. But one pious man alone adjured him in God's name to pronounce no such sentence for his crops; adding that he was right well content that the poor should take from him in their need, and that he commended to the Lord's care whatsoever was left.
>
> Now scarcely had the priest perforce begun the curse, than there suddenly arose such a storm of thunder, lightning, whirl-wind, rain and hail, that the corn in the fields was torn from the ground as by a blast from hell; and all that grew therein, and the cattle, and the very birds, were destroyed, as though trodden down by carts and horses. But that just man found his land without trace of harm. And thus it is clear that as the angels sing Glory to God in the Highest, so on earth is there Peace toward men of Good-will.
>
> This storm began on the borders of Bedfordshire (at Eltisley) and passed eastwards through the Isle of Ely. And here is a wondrous thing. Such crops as still stood when it was over were found so rotted that neither horse nor ass, steer nor pig, goose nor hen, would eat thereof (quotation in Coneybeare).

Among Eltisley's more notorious families is the Desborough (Disbrowe) family and in particular the two brothers John (1608–80) and Samuel (1619–90). John, nicknamed 'the grim Gyant Desborough' and married to Oliver Cromwell's sister Jane, had, at least initially, a distinguished military career as a captain, colonel and major-general. In 1654 he became MP for Cambridgeshire and in 1656 for Somerset. He was, however, cashiered in 1659, shortly after which he was imprisoned on suspicion of plotting to kill Charles II and his mother, Queen Henrietta Maria. On his release he fled to Holland. After obeying a proclamation requiring him to return to England, in 1666 he was imprisoned again for intrigue in Holland. After a year he was released and remained free until his death in Hackney.

Samuel left England in 1639 with another Cambridgeshire man, William Lete of Doddington, for the Americas. In 1641 they were among some of the original settlers of Guildford, Connecticut. While William stayed on to become a colonial statesman and governor, Samuel returned during the Civil War to become MP for Midlothian and Edinburgh. After the restoration of the monarchy he accepted the king's declaration of pardon.

Eltisley centres on a remarkably attractive and classic English green. The setting for many quintessentially English village cricket matches, it is overlooked by the parish church with its slender Midland spire, and surrounded by elegant houses, a pub and old trees. Among the houses is a late medieval hall house and probably the oldest house, Old Post Office, dating to about 1612. Of five former inns, only the Leeds Arms (*c*. 1814), remains; it is where for about a hundred years inquests were regularly held. Three chestnut trees, known as Faith, Hope, and Charity, were planted in 1877 to commemorate Queen Victoria's Golden Jubilee. A long row of trees, the Row of Honour, commemorates those of Eltisley who fell in the First World War and in March 1919 the evergreen Peace Tree was planted at the head of the line. On the edge of the cricket ground, the village sign depicts the church and St Pandionia on one side and on the other a village cricket match.

The young Bourn Brook flows east and south-east towards Caxton, meaning Kakkr's homestead, passing the ancient site of Caxton Moats. It is the site of a large moated fortification built in the early to mid-twelfth century by King Stephen. It may have been part of a number of similar fortifications, for example Horsey Hill Fort near Peterborough, Giant's Hill near Rampton, and at Burwell Castle, all built by King Stephen to contain rebels, particularly Geoffrey de Mandeville, who was eventually killed by Stephen at the unfinished castle at Burwell (see chapter 12). Possibly as a result of this victory the lives of all these forts were short-lived and by the middle of the thirteenth century they were ineffective as forts or castles. By the late thirteenth century the estate of Caxton Moats had passed to the widow Eleanor de Freville, mother of the heir to the de Scalers' estate.

As might have been expected, Caxton did not grow up along the Roman Ermine Street, particularly as it was crossed here by other Roman ways including the Lot Way. Instead, the original Anglo-Saxon settlement of Caustone was established to the south-west of the present village, around its parish church of St Andrew which, although essentially late thirteenth century, contains a few Saxon fragments. The nearby narrow lanes and scattered finds of medieval pottery indicate quite a widespread settlement.

As traffic along Ermine Street increased, so the village gradually moved alongside. A market was granted in 1247. It lasted into the eighteenth century and its site is the open space in the middle of the village opposite Caxton Manor. After the new stone bridge had been built in Huntingdon in 1332, traffic increased even more and as time went by almost all the village was concentrated alongside Ermine Street, or as it was now known the Old North Road, and one of the first turnpike roads in Britain. Not only did Caxton become a small market town, but it also became a staging post and post town. Its importance is reflected in a number of large houses, all once coaching inns. These include the Crown (fifteenth century), Caxton Manor (late sixteenth century and formerly the George Inn), the Cross Keys (the site on which an inn of the same name still stands) and Red Lion Farm (sixteenth to seventeenth century). The windows of these inns were let to Cambridge undergraduates to watch the Young Pretender go by during the Jacobite Rising. Unfortunately for the students he never got as far south.

By the mid-seventeenth century there was a county tollgate here: it only lasted five years as traffic quickly learnt to bypass it on the old roads to the west by the church. Despite this, however, Caxton's importance continued to grow and it is noteworthy that in Badeslade and Tom's map of 1742, apart from Cambridge and Ely, only six towns of special significance are shown; one of them is Caxton. Perhaps this was because the post office established in the early seventeenth century was, in the mid-eighteenth century, the only post office in the county outside Cambridge. In 1753 mail was carried twice a week by horseback between Caxton and Cambridge, the only mail connection the city had other than with London and Bury St Edmunds.

*Caxton Gibbet.*

Although Caxton has the look of a traditional coaching town, as a village straddling a major road, it has none of the charms of the surrounding villages, such as Eltisley. Its inhabitants were mainly labourers and innkeepers and it was described as mean and shoddy:

> Thence to poor Caxton I was led in
> To a poor house, poorer bedding.
>                     R. Braithwaite, 1638 (quotation in Palmer).

While Caxton definitely does not include William Caxton, who was born in Kent, among its sons, some say the Benedictine monk and Chronicler of St Albans, Matthew Paris (d. 1259), was born in the village. While he had the reputation of being one of the best early English chroniclers, he was also an expert mathematician, architect, artist, poet and jeweller. He was employed, among other things, in the reformation of abuses which were prevalent in various monasteries at that time.

Caxton also had a very sinister side – its own gibbet. Its unlikely first owners were the abbots of Ramsey, and it was not until the dissolution that it became the property of the Crown. The present gallows standing at the crossroads of Ermine Street and the Cambridge to St Neots road, at the junction of four parishes, is a replica. However, its site, albeit somewhat altered in the 1980s, is the original medieval one. Here sheep stealers, petty thieves, highwaymen and murderers met their end, often suspended in iron cages until they died.

One such highwayman was the amateur highwayman Gatward, who was known on the north road between Royston and Huntingdon. In due time he was caught, tried and sentenced to death; he was hung and gibbeted at Caxton. A contemporary account describes how he was 'hanged in chains . . . in a scarlet coat, and after he had hung about two or three months it is supposed that the screw was filed which supported him and that he fell in the first high wind after . . . it was a great grief to his mother' (quotation in Harper). His mother, a Royston innkeeper, secretly conveyed his body to her inn where he was given a decent but unconsecrated burial in the cellar.

An account is given (in Porter) of a man called Partridge who in 1836 murdered a young girl at Monkfield Farm (half a mile to the north-east of Caxton and now subsumed by Cambourn). He avoided detection and escaped to America. Years later he returned, visited the scene of his crime and then went on to drink in one of the Caxton inns. The drink got the better of him and as he started to boast about his various exploits the landlord became suspicious. He called the police and Partridge, identified by a birthmark, was arrested. In due course he was placed alive in one of the iron cages that was then strung up from the gibbet. It was said that a passing baker took pity on him and gave him a loaf of bread. For this kindly act the baker was later hanged from the same gibbet.

A notable feature of some of the older roads in the country is the presence of wide, open verges. In part this may stem directly from the murder of two thirteenth-century merchants on a nearby stretch of Ermine Street in Bourn Wood. Consequently, in an

*Bourn Windmill.*

attempt to protect travellers, it was ordered that all roadside banks be levelled, ditches filled in, bushes cleared and trees cut down, so as to destroy the hiding places of robbers and murderers.

The brook continues on its way south-east from Caxton towards the village which gave it its name: Bourn. As it does so it passes Bourn Windmill, the finest post mill in the county and one of the best in the country. Such mills, the designs of which date from the twelfth century, derive their name from the massive upright post which supports the wooden-framed weather-boarded body of the mill itself. The body is turned around this post to face the wind by a long wooden tiller. Although none of the medieval mills have survived, Bourn Mill claims to be the second oldest in England, and there is documentary evidence that there was a mill on this site before 1636, when it was apparently bought and sold by deed.

Bourn, from Brunna, meaning a stream or brook, is divided by that very same brook. To the north, lying close to the line of the Lot Way, are the somewhat grandly titled Moulton Hills. Excavations carried out in 1909 yielded many Roman artefacts including human bones, indicating that the 'hills' were originally burial mounds. The excavations also revealed Saxon pottery and medieval millstones, which suggest that there may once have been considerable activity here and in all probability a windmill on one of the mounds.

In the ninth century land to the south belonged to the lordship of Morcar, 'who had a numerous and warlike family, but he and most of them were killed by the Danes'. It was in 870 that, according to the Parker Chronicle, 'the host rode across Mercia into East Anglia . . . and the same year King Edmund fought against them, and the Danes won the victory, and they slew the King and overran the entire kingdom'.

William the Conqueror subsequently gave this land to his sheriff Picot (Pigot), and it was he who built, on a low hill overlooking Ermine Street, a Norman castle. It consisted of a circular rampart containing a chapel, a bailey and surrounding defensive banks and ditches.

After a succession of owners, in the sixteenth century the site passed to the wealthy local family of Haggar. It was this family, which had made its fortune in the wool trade, that built in the middle of the earthworks that had previously surrounded the castle the late Elizabethan Bourn Hall. In its turn the hall too passed through the hands of many owners, among which were the Leyalls and their heirs, the Earls de la Warr (Delawarr). The earls rebuilt much of the house using materials, including woodwork, a staircase and a chimney piece, from the ruinous Haslingfield Hall. More works were carried out in the nineteenth century. Indeed, so many works had been carried out that in 1817 it was described as 'being more Elizabethan' than the original and in 1851 as 'a tasteful imitation of the Elizabethan style'. In 1985 the hall became internationally known as the Bourn Hall clinic which pioneered work on test-tube babies, a far cry indeed from Sheriff Picot's Norman castle.

Turning gradually to the east the brook flows between Caldecote and Kingston. From the north bank it is overlooked by Caldecote's parish church of St Mary which had been sited about half a mile south of the early medieval hill-land and woodland settlement. Originally the village was an outlying hamlet of Bourn and as such only had a 'capella'. It was not until the twelfth century that it was recognised as a parish in its own right. Immediately opposite, Kingston's fourteenth-century parish church of All Saints and St Andrew, but much repaired in 1488 following a fire, overlooks the brook from the south bank. Inside are some remarkable medieval wall paintings depicting two armed knights attacking, on horseback, angels and the cross, the Wheel of Fortune, St Christopher, and some sixteenth-century inscriptions with arabesques. The original settlement, where Roman and late Iron Age fragments have been found, would have been near the church and the medieval Old Rectory, overlooking the brook.

While neither Caldecote nor Kingston are strictly valley villages, the Bourn Brook and small tributaries flow through and around Toft, half a mile to the east. The original settlement lay on either side of the brook; the church was sited on the Lot

Way. One of the earliest references to Toft, meaning simply a small farmstead or homestead, is about the purchase of lands in Toft in 970 by Abbot Brithnorth of Ely and Bishop Aethelwold of Winchester for the Monastery of Ely.

Its stone church, dating from the mid-fourteenth century and possibly standing on the site of an earlier wooden church, was somewhat unsympathetically rebuilt in the late nineteenth century. It had suffered some 200 years earlier at the hands of William Dowsing (1596?–1679?). A formidable iconoclast who became the Parliamentary Visitor of Suffolk, he had been similarly employed in Cambridgeshire where an eyewitness in 1643 described him as having 'battered and beaten downe all our painted glasse' (quotation in CDNB). At Toft, however, he did not confine his attentions to the glass. Even though he did destroy twenty-seven pictures in the windows, he also destroyed the alabaster reredos, removed St Christopher's hands and decapitated St Hubert, the patron saint of hunters, who had been given a key by St Peter with which to cure hydrophobia. For that 'purification' he was paid 6s 8d. Given the surname of Dowsing (meaning water divining), could there have been any significance in the decapitation, or alternatively the fact that he left the key?

Flowing generally east from Toft, the brook crosses the Greenwich Meridian (commemorated by a roadside sundial in the village) to run beside the travelling telescope of the Mullard Radio Astronomy Observatory. Just downstream from

*The Bourn Brook near the Mullard Radio Astronomy Observatory.*

*The Bourn Brook near Cantelupe Farm, upstream from Byron's Pool.*

Lord's Bridge, where there had been an Iron Age settlement and where cremation urns and amphorae were found in the nineteenth century, it is joined by a small tributary, the Tit Brook, which rises in and around Comberton.

The name Comberton is one of the few Celtic place names in the county and is derived from Cumberton (as it is presently pronounced) or Cumbrian's Ton, the Welshman's or Briton's farm. Lands were anciently held from the Crown by Philip de Hastings through service, not as a knight but as keeper of the king's falcon. In the reign of Edward I half a hide* was held by 'the grand serjeantry of being the King's baker'. William the Conqueror started the practice when he required the baker to make a simnel cake daily; in Edward's reign the frequency was reduced to one cake per week.

At the north end of the village is the moated site of the manor house, which dated from the early thirteenth century. It was to become Green's Manor House after Sir Henry Green (d. 1369). A judge of common pleas and later chief justice of the King's Bench, he was excommunicated by the pope in 1358 for sentencing Bishop Thomas Lisle (d. 1361) who had fallen out with the daughter of Henry, Earl of Lancaster. The bishop was compelled to flee and died as a refugee in Avignon.

To the south is the site of another manor, Burdely's Manor. Through marriage, it later formed part of Sheriff Picot's estate. While there are no remains, the lands, having passed through the hands of the Bishop of Winchester in the sixteenth century, are subject to the governors of St Thomas Hospital as current lords of the manor.

Between the two manors was a maze. Mazes were popular as early as the sixteenth century and had a special significance, probably religious, for the local inhabitants. It is suggested (by Burton) that the maze represents the journey through life. The entrance represents birth; the centre paradise. On the way, wrong turns correspond to sins and as the path becomes more complex towards the centre, it mirrors the increasing complexity of life.

The Comberton Maze, which possibly dates from the sixteenth century, was about 50ft in diameter with tracks about 3ft wide divided by small turf banks about 1ft high. A late nineteenth-century guidebook describes the 'curious ancient maze in front of the National School. It has been paved with pebbles, but is, no doubt, of great antiquity.' While it was clearly visible in the early twentieth century, it had been given to the care of the school and was finally, and sadly, covered over in 1926.

Still flowing to the east, the Bourn Brook forms the southern boundary of Barton parish, and passes close by Bird's Farm House, which probably dates to the 1440s, and is the oldest house in the village. After a pretty stretch, unfortunately dominated by the M11 motorway, the brook joins the River Cam in the calm of Byron's Pool.

* A hide was an area of land thought sufficient to support a single family, approximately between 60 and 120 acres.

# 7

# *The Poets' River*

Arguably the stretch of the River Cam between Byron's Pool and Queen's Bridge in Cambridge is both the most romantic and notorious of the whole river. Lord Byron swam in 'The sleepy pool above the dam, The pool beneath it never still.' The River Cam and the Bourn Brook join at Byron's Pool. A wide, sometimes gloomy and brooding pool surrounded by nettles, brambles and ivy-covered trees in damp earth, it is nevertheless a tranquil spot favoured by many poets including Lord Byron, who is said to haunt the banks. While he was up at Trinity College, he preferred this spot above others for swimming. He was an accomplished swimmer having once swum some 3 miles of the Thames under both Blackfriars and Westminster Bridges.

However, during the seventeenth century he would have found it difficult to practise his sport. According to Coneybeare, during the Puritan ascendancy Cambridge University made an enactment to the effect that 'if any student should by day or night enter any river, ditch, lake, pond, mere or any other water within the County of Cambridge, whether for the sake of swimming or of washing, he should be flogged in his college hall'. This was followed by a second flogging carried out at the university schools by the proctors. For any subsequent offence he would have been expelled.

Alfred Lord Tennyson, possibly accompanied by a miller's daughter, wrote:

> From the bridge . . . leaned to hear
> The mill dam rushing down with noise
> And see the minnows dancing everywhere
> In crystal eddies glance and poise.

Geoffrey Chaucer wrote:

> At Trompyngtoun, nat far fro Canterbrigge,
> There goth a brook and over that a brigge.
> Upon the whiche brook ther stant a melle,
> And this is verray soth that I you tell.

A thought echoed by Rupert Brooke:

> Beside the pleasant mill of Trumpington
> I laughed with Chaucer in the hawthorn glade.

*Byron's Pool.*

In spite of ruins reported in 1819, the exact site of Trumpington Mill is not known. It may have stood just above Byron's Pool, which was actually its mill pool. However, it is more likely that the pool is natural, simply being formed at the junction of the two rivers. That being so, the site of Grantchester Mill, where there has been a mill for centuries, is the more likely site of Chaucer's 'melle'. Following a fire the present mill dates from 1902.

A little before Chaucer's time Matthew Paris wrote about Trumpington in 1259:

A youth who passing through Trumpington, threw a stone at a dog and killed an old woman's hen. She refused compensation and complained to William de Bussey, Seneschal [steward] of William de Valence uterine brother of Henry the Third. He threw the youth into prison where he died. The priest of Trumpington, having found the body thrown on a dung-hill, gave it a Christian burial. William de Bussey had it disinterred and hung on a gibbet. Such was justice in the evil days of Henry the Third (quotation in Murray).

In the Church of St Mary and St Michael, parts of which date from about 1200, but severely restored by Butterfield in 1876, is a tomb with the famous brass effigy of Sir Roger de Trumpington (d. 1289). It is the second oldest brass in England, the only known earlier one being that of Sir John D'Abernon at Stoke D'Abernon in Surrey, dated 1277. The brass, which was mounted on Purbeck marble and depicting a knight over 6ft tall in armour, his helmet shackled to his belt and his sword held by his dog, was originally made for his father, Sir Giles de Trumpington. Sir Roger, who had served in the crusades in about 1270 with the future Edward I, predeceased his father Sir Giles, who decided to alter it to suit his son.

Two of Trumpington's later sons were born within a year of each other. George Henty (1832–1902), received his education at Westminster and Caius College, Cambridge, before serving in the Crimea with the hospital commissariat. While he was still serving he took up journalism reporting on the Austro-Italian War, from Abyssinia, on the Franco-German War, from Ashanti, and from the Prince of Wales's Indian tour. In 1868 he started writing his adventure books for boys. His first publication was *Out of the Pampas* and, drawing on his experience, it was followed by some three books per year until his death in 1902.

A year later Henry Fawcett (1833–84) was born. When he was only twenty-five he was accidentally blinded while out shooting with his short-sighted father. He resolved that this should not alter his planned life. He maintained his fellowship at Trinity Hall in Cambridge and was appointed professor of Political Economy in 1863. He became the Liberal MP for Brighton and from his deep interest in Indian affairs was known as 'The member for India'. In 1880 he was made postmaster-general and was responsible for parcel post, postal orders and telegrams. Despite being blind he was an accomplished fisherman, fearsome horseman, tireless pedestrian and remarkable skater. He said, 'Do not patronise those who are blind, treat us without reference to our misfortune; and above all help us to be independent.' In 1867 he married Millicent Garrett (1847–1929) from Aldeburgh, younger sister of Elizabeth Garrett and one of the first advocates of votes for women. Widowed at only thirty-seven she worked tirelessly to promote women's rights, becoming president of the National Union of Women's Suffrage Societies in 1897 and a dame in 1925.

Mee tells a tale of the unfortunate naturalist Dr F.H.H. Guillemard, one of whose ancestors came over from France, not with William the Conqueror but in a ward-robe, as a Huguenot escaping persecution. The wardrobe was still in the house when the doctor died; however, his mother when spring-cleaning had burnt his pile of three-cornered Cape stamps that he had collected as a boy. Little did she realise how very valuable they would have become.

Trumpington became the home of the Plant Breeding Institute founded in 1912 by Sir Rowland Henry Biffin FRS (1874–1949). In 1908 Sir Henry was appointed Professor of Agricultural Botany at Cambridge and was Director of the Institute from 1912 until his retirement in 1936, having concentrated specifically on wheat, barley oats and peas. The institute became independent of the university after the

Second World War, when it moved to Trumpington. Plant breeding was transformed to an orderly scientific method, and among its successes has been the development of the Maris family of potatoes such as Maris Peer (1963), Maris Page (1965) and the well-known Maris Piper (1965).

Noteworthy houses in Trumpington include the sixteenth-century timber-framed Green Man Inn and Anstey Hall, built in about 1700, which had passed to the Anstey family later in the eighteenth century. The hall, rebuilt in the seventeenth century on the site of an earlier manor house, was the early home of another distinguished poet, Christopher Anstey (1724–1805), who had translated Gray's *Elegy* into Latin and who published the *New Bath Guide* in 1766. On the other side of the road is the home of the Pemberton family, Trumpington Hall. Between the twelfth and sixteenth centuries the Trumpington family held this manor. Like Anstey Hall, this hall was built on the site of a much earlier manor, possibly thirteenth century. While it was reconstructed in the eighteenth century and further modified in the twentieth century it contains some Jacobean panelling.

Early Iron Age settlements were often placed in pairs; Trumpington and Grantchester across the river form just such a pair. Whether this Poets' Corner would have become quite so famous without one particular poet is questionable. As Rupert Brooke recalled in the Café des Westens in Berlin in May 1912:

> In Grantchester, in Grantchester . . .
> Still in the dawn lit waters cool
> His ghostly Lordship swims his pool . . .
>
> But Grantchester! Ah, Grantchester!
> There's peace and holy quiet there . . .

And went on to observe

> Dan Chaucer hears his river still
> Chatter beneath a phantom mill.
> Tennyson notes with studious eye
> How Cambridge waters hurry by.

The son of a Rugby schoolmaster, Rupert Brooke was known for his beauty, which he regarded very highly; however, the homosexual circles within which he moved soon became too oppressive. He began to receive unwanted attention consequent upon a certain form of deviant behaviour, which he called a 'pretty affectation'. These attentions and jealousies, together with an unsatisfactory love affair with Katherine Cox of Newnham, nearly caused him to have a nervous breakdown. To escape and recover he moved to the seventeenth-century Old Vicarage in Grantchester, which he made his second home. Lord Byron was not the only poet to swim in Byron's Pool; allegedly Brooke and the novelist Virginia Woolf swam there together, naked. He died of an infected mosquito bite on his way to

*Rupert Brooke statue at the Old Vicarage.*

Gallipoli at Skyros in 1915. He was buried there, in 'a corner of some foreign field that is forever England'.

The origin of the name Grantchester is confusing. The early river name here was the Granta and hence the village began as Granteseta, 'the settlers by the Granta'. The 'chester', from the Latin *castra* (camp or walled town), was most likely introduced in error in about 1200. However, while there was a large Romano-British house here, there was no walled town at Grantchester. This name led to confusion with Grantabridge, Cantabridge, Caumbridge and finally Cambridge where there had been a walled town.

The early lords of the manor were the Provost and Fellows of King's College, Cambridge, later to become Rupert Brooke's college. During the plague of the seventeenth century they and the rest of the college sought refuge in their manor house. According to a tradition (told by Porter) two passages lead from the manor house's cellar, one of which is said to extend to King's College Chapel. A musician wished to prove this and he set off down the passage, the ceiling of which became lower and lower. As he went he played his fiddle that initially sounded 'loud and clear'. As he progressed further the noise became quieter and quieter until it faded away completely. The fiddler was never seen again. An eighteenth-century bursar of King's College called one of the fields nearby Fiddler's Close.

*Grantchester Mill Pool.*

On the tower of the Church of St Andrew and St Mary, standing on the site of a Norman or late Saxon church, is a curious piece of iron. It was put there in 1823 to help the astronomical work of Cambridge, standing as it does exactly south of the old university observatory, 2½ miles away. Following the introduction of self-collimating telescopes in 1869 it ceased to be of value and anyway surrounding trees had made the tower invisible from the observatory.

Grantchester was said in 1968 'to be a place of recreation and retirement for the students and scholars of Cambridge . . . some of the smaller buildings put up between 1715 and 1850 are not without academic overtones' (quotation in Scarfe), and it is certainly a place of recreation for the thousands who have been there on foot, in a skiff or a punt, for breakfast after a Cambridge May Ball, lunch in one of the three inns, tea at the famous Orchard Tea Rooms or just for a riverside picnic. Although Grantchester has attained a new notoriety through the present incumbent of the Old Vicarage, the politician and author Jeffrey Archer, it is still fitting to say:

> Stands the Church clock at ten to three?
> And is there honey still for tea?

As the river flows towards Cambridge, William Wordsworth found it difficult to lightly sleep beside it. Milton, however, found it easy:

> . . . the waters murmuring
> With such consort as they keep,
> Entice the dewy-feathered Sleep.

There were sometimes surprises on the way. In 1909 Augustus John came to Cambridge to paint a portrait of the classical Greek scholar Jane Harrison (1850–1928) of Newnham College. Rather than staying in Cambridge he chose to camp at Grantchester Meadows with two wives and ten naked mud-spattered children apparently chewing on stones for their supper. Boating parties from Cambridge were arranged so that the university dons could see this amazing sight.

On the west bank of the river between Grantchester and Cambridge is a water meadow called Lingay Fen. In severe winters this would be flooded and lit in the evening and at night by old gas street lights. It became a favourite venue for skaters and drew both genteel and elegant figure skaters and hardened and athletic Fenland skaters. In the late nineteenth century both the Amateur and Professional Skating Championships of Great Britain were held here. Among those who took part in the Professional Championships were the legendary Welney friends and rivals William 'Turkey' Smart, who in 1870 skated faster than the King's Lynn to London train between Littleport and Ely, his nephew George 'Fish' Smart and William 'Gutta Percha' See. On rare occasions the entire river would freeze over and it was possible to skate from Cambridge to Ely. In the evenings the banks of The Backs were lit with lanterns and candles; in the daytime all of Cambridge and his wife would be on the ice. Arguably there was better skating on the many acres of ice at the old Cambridge sewage works. Skaters soon learnt not to fall down too heavily!

By the early nineteenth century rules for swimming had been relaxed and, closer to Cambridge, public and university swimming sheds were built. Gwen Raverat recalls that, for boys at least, there were no such things as swimming costumes. This could cause both amusement and embarrassment to Victorian and Edwardian ladies on their way to river picnics.

Some of these boys could have been from the King's Choir School who from the 1830s had to demonstrate their swimming capabilities by passing a series of tests. In the mid-twentieth century their introduction to swimming started in an old car tyre suspended in a large bath tub by a pulley and rope held by a master, often the head-master. When the pupil could float he progressed to the 'Little River' on Sheeps' Green Fen, a nearby tributary that ran parallel to the River Cam. When he could swim across and back he was allowed to swim in the 'Big River'.

Sheeps' Green, the fen lying between the Little River and the Big River, with the Leys public school to the east, has to be one of the most accurately delineated areas in the county if not the country. It is the area where generations of engineering students have first learnt their surveying skills. The red-brick Leys School was founded by the Wesleyans in 1875, much being designed by the architect Sir Aston Webb (1849–1930).

So the two branches of the river continue and join at the mill by Queens' College Bridge. From at least the time of Domesday until 1928 there were two mills on the

*King's and Bishop's Mill Pool.*

main branch of the river, the King's Mill built by Sheriff Picot and the Bishop's Mill, belonging to the Abbot of Ely. On the lesser branch of the river was a third mill, Newnham Mill. Presently, punts and rowing boats can be hired at either mill pool for use on the 'upper' river, above the old mill weirs and the 'lower' river along the Backs.

There is, however, another river that rises above Cambridge at Nine Wells between Trumpington and Great Shelford. Nine is not a definite number and its source is actually a series of springs. In the sixteenth century this river, the Vicar's Brook, flowed across the Cambridge to London road at Trumpington, where there was a ford, and thence to the River Cam, but its course was to be changed.

In 1573 an outbreak of the plague in Cambridge led to a suggestion by Archbishop Matthew Parker that water be conveyed from the Trumpington ford to scour and clean the King's Ditch and to bring fresh water into the town. This ditch, of which there is now no obvious trace, dates from the Danish occupation and was remade by King John and Henry III. While its main purpose may have been protective, it failed to keep out the barons and Geoffrey de Mandeville (d. 1144) from the fens. It ran from Newnham Mill, the King's Mill, as far east as Christ's College before turning back along Hobson Street to rejoin the River Cam opposite Magdalene College like a town moat. For centuries it formed the eastern boundary of the city. It was also used as a water carrier and common sewer; 'once made to defend Cambridge by its strength, did in its time offend it with its stench'. It was filled in, none too soon, in the nineteenth century.

At about the same time the master of Peterhouse College, Dr Andrew Perne (1519?–89), made a similar suggestion to the chancellor of the university. Dr Perne, while being Dean of Ely, had such accommodating views on religion that he survived the ups and downs of the Reformation unscathed. As a Protestant in Edward VI's reign he destroyed almost every book in the University Library as he considered them to be idolatrous. Serving Queen Mary he dug up and publicly burnt the bodies of the Protestant teachers Martin Bucer (1491–1551) and Paul Fagius (1504–49). Under Elizabeth he became convinced again that Protestantism was the only true form of religion. University wits of the time coined a new Latin verb, *pernare*, meaning a turncoat. These wits also declared that the initials A.P. on the weathervane that he gave to his college stood for A Protestant or A Papist as appropriate.

Nothing was done for about thirty years until 1606 when Thomas Hobson (1544?–1631) and a group of 'undertakers' or investors changed the course of the Vicar's Brook and introduced water via Hobson's Brook, sometimes called the New Little River, into Cambridge for drinking, street cleaning and scouring the drains, its cost being shared by the university and the town. On its way it fed the University Botanic Gardens that had been founded in 1761 by Dr Walker, vice-master of Trinity College, and moved from the middle of Cambridge to its present site on the Trumpington Road in 1846. At the river's head or conduit, it branched out into three watercourses. While there was insufficient water to scour the King's Ditch, one branch provided drinking water at a fountain in Market Hill from 1614 to 1856. This fountain, an ornamented stone hexagonal 'pepper pot' crowned with a gilded fir cone

*Hobson's Conduit.*

and now known as Hobson's Conduit, was moved to the conduit head in 1856. On it is the inscription 'Thomas Hobson Carrier between Cambridge and London a great Benefactore to this University Town. Died January 1st 1630 in the 86th yeare of his age. This structure stood on the Market Hill and served as a conduit from 1614 to 1856 in which year it was re-erected on this spot by public subscription.'

It was replaced by an arched and gabled Gothic-style fountain. Another branch of the conduit fed runlets along the gutters of St Andrew's Street and Trinity Street and the third branch fed the ponds in the Emmanuel College and Christ's College gardens. In 1689, during William III's visit to Cambridge, the conduit was made to run with wine. The wine only cost 30*d* and was apparently 'not very good'.

Thomas Hobson's father, who died in 1568, was treasurer of the Cambridge Corporation. He bequeathed land in Grantchester to his son Thomas (1568–1631) as well as the wagons and horses that Thomas had been driving for his father. As a local carrier being specially licensed to trade between Cambridge and London, he held the monopoly as he plied his trade with large six- and eight-horse wagons, the journey in which would take three days or more. He carried not only goods but also passengers. He also kept a large stable with some forty horses that he would let out for hire. He even provided boots and whips for the journey. While his business was prosperous, he became very autocratic. He never allowed any horse to be chosen by a customer; he decided. His decision was based on the work the horse had recently done and its position in the stable. 'This or none' he would say, which expression gave rise to the well-known saying 'It is Hobson's Choice'.

He became Mayor of Cambridge and left money for charities including the Spinning House, or Hobson's Workhouse, that he had founded in 1628 to provide shelter and employment for the hard-up and a correction centre for the 'stubborn rogues'. It was also used as the vice-chancellor's prison for prostitutes. The building stood until 1901 when it was replaced by the former borough police station in Regent Street. Thomas died on 1 January 1631 and was buried, without a memorial, in the chancel of St Bene't's Church.

At his death John Milton was a young man aged twenty-three. In a rare moment of good humour he wrote some uncharacteristic 'undergraduate' humorous verses (which were not particularly funny) about the Cambridge carrier.

> On the University Carrier, who sickened in
> the time of the Vacancy, being forbid to
> go to London by reason of the Plague.
>
> Here lies old Hobson; Death hath broke his girt,
> And here, alas! hath laid him in the dirt;
> Or else, the ways being foul, twenty to one
> He's stuck in a slough, and overthrown.
> 'Twas such a shifter that, if truth were known,
> Death was half glad when he had got him down;
> For he had any time this ten years full
> Dodged with him betwixt Cambridge and the Bull. . . .

On the edge of the King's and Bishop's Mill pool is the late eighteenth-century former home of the artist and author Gwen Raverat (1885–1957), Newnham Grange. Well known for her evocative book on her Cambridge childhood, *Period Piece* (1952), she was the daughter of the mathematician Sir George Howard Darwin (1845–1912) and granddaughter of Charles Darwin (1809–82). In 1964 it became Darwin College, a small college of graduate students, and an unfortunate octagonal dining room on stilts was incorporated into the building. The same architects designed the nearby University Centre, situated, also unfortunately, by the riverside on the site of the former King's and Bishop's Mills.

Leaving the Mill Pool, the River Cam flows under Silver Street Bridge and passes through The Backs.

# 8

# *A Morning Perambulation*

While many see the quiet beauty of Cambridge from the River Cam in a punt, perhaps chauffeured, there is probably no other city in the world where such an unrivalled variety of architecture and history can be seen and sensed while on a walk of just half a mile. The walk, parallel with the river, starts at Hobson's Conduit and proceeds along Trumpington Street, King's Parade, Trinity Street, St John's Street and Bridge Street finishing back at the River Cam at 'The Great Bridge' and Magdalene College.

The modern façade of the Judge Institute of Management Studies on the east side of the street hides the Old Addenbrooke's Hospital. Dr John Addenbrooke (1680–1719), a fellow of St Catherine's College who had practised in Cambridge, bequeathed about £5,000 to fund a small hospital in the town. Initially there was an apothecary, a matron, four nurses and some twelve beds. Despite severe financial difficulties it expanded rapidly during the nineteenth century and was rebuilt in 1863 to designs by Sir Mathew Digby Wyatt (1820–77), the first Slade Professor of Fine Arts in Cambridge. By this time it had become a teaching hospital with some 1,000 patients. In 1966 the hospital, by then famous throughout the world, moved to a new site on the southern outskirts of Cambridge where it dominates the skyline.

On the other side of the street is possibly the finest classical building which has been built of late years in the country: the Fitzwilliam Museum or as it is known locally, the Fitzbilly or simply the Fitz. Richard Fitzwilliam (1745–1816), the 7th Viscount Fitzwilliam of Meryon, bequeathed £100,000 to the university to build a museum that would also house his collection of books, prints, paintings and manuscripts. A university syndicate was appointed to look after his bequest and carry out his wishes. The syndicate was not exactly fast in progressing the matter and the collection was initially housed in a disused part of the Perse School. First, King's College was asked to sell the whole of its Kings Parade frontage (which at that date had not been built upon). The request was very firmly rebuffed, as was a similar request to St Catherine's College for the site of the old Bull Hotel. Other unsuccessful suggestions included the Senate House Yard, between Great St Mary's and St Michael's Churches and on the frontage of Gonville and Caius. In 1823 the syndicate eventually persuaded Peterhouse College to sell part of its site. However, having obtained the land nothing was done for the next eleven years, at which time, 1834, the Perse School announced that it required the space taken up by the collection. It was moved to part of the University Library where it stayed until 1848.

*Fitzwilliam Museum.*

The move from the Perse finally forced the syndicate to take action and a competition for the design of a suitable building was announced. A neo-classical design, Roman more than Greek, by the architect George Basevi (1794–1845) was finally chosen and construction started in 1837. Work proceeded slowly until 1845 when Basevi fell down inside the west tower of Ely Cathedral and was killed. The architect Charles Cockerell (1788–1863) completed the building in 1845 and, as one of the best examples of 'museum architecture' in the country, it is a fitting memorial to George Basevi. The main body of the museum and the later extensions house a world-famous collection which includes paintings of the Dutch and Flemish School, English landscape and Impressionist paintings, books, armour, weapons, Egyptian artefacts, prints, pottery and porcelain.

In January 2006 Nick Flynn, a frequent visitor to the museum, tripped on his shoelace and fell down a flight of marble stairs. On his way down he demolished three of five Qing dynasty porcelain vases valued at some £300,000. They had been standing on the same shelf for many years but had now been reduced to thousands of pieces. Despite this, restoration in the shape of three, three-dimensional, jigsaw puzzles started and the least damaged was repaired by the following June.

Opposite the museum is a gently curving terrace, Fitzwilliam Street. Largely unchanged since the early nineteenth century, here were the homes of Charles Kingsley and, after his voyage in the *Beagle*, Charles Darwin. Fitzwilliam House, built in 1727, was bought for the university in 1887 and reconstituted as a 'Day Boy House' for students unattached to any college. It fulfilled a need, as since 1869 every member of the university had to belong to a college. It was the last college to be established in Cambridge during the nineteenth century; it removed to new buildings on the Huntingdon Road in 1963.

Walking along this section of Trumpington Street it is easy to imagine a story that has probably been told countless times about many academics. Murray tells one version concerning a Professor Robert Seely, professor of Modern History from 1869 to 1895. Walking past the conduit one day deep in thought 'a mischievous boy switched a copious shower of water over him from the little stream in the gutter'. Still deep in thought he immediately unfurled his umbrella and so continued his walk home.

In 1280 Hugh de Balsham (d. 1286), Bishop of Ely from 1257 to 1286, obtained a charter from Edward I to introduce some secular scholars into the Hospital of

*Peterhouse College.*

St John that had been founded by townsmen in about 1200. In so doing, Hugh, a Benedictine, was attempting to combine secular and religious interests. It did not work; they could not live together and they quarrelled and fought. In 1284 Hugh moved his scholars as far away as possible to two hostels belonging to a lesser order of friars, the Friars of the Sack, in the parish of St Peter just outside the town's Trumpington Gate, thus founding the House of St Peter or as it was to become known Peterhouse, the earliest college in Cambridge. In about 1307 the friars were suppressed and the college obtained their lands and house. Hugh had modelled the college, with its master and scholars, on Merton College which had been established in Oxford in 1274 by Walter de Merton, Bishop of Rochester. The college was to be secular and non-monastic in character, its first statutes being laid down by Hugh and his successor at Ely, Simon de Montacute (d. 1345) in 1338. There was to be provision for a master and fourteen fellows who were to be 'engaged in the pursuit of literature [and] so far as human frailty admit be honourable, chaste, peaceable, humble and modest'. Additionally, however, 'The Master and all and each of the scholars of our house shall adopt the clerical dress and tonsure . . . and not allow their beards or their hair to grow contrary to canonical prohibition, not to wear rings on their fingers for their own vain glory and boasting' (quotations in Reeve).

The college's hall, built in about 1286, while greatly restored, is the oldest part of the building and, with its medieval stonework, the earliest part of a collegiate building in Cambridge. The two original houses were pulled down in about 1630 to make way for the college's chapel. For nearly four centuries members of the college worshipped in the neighbouring Church of St Peter which dates from the twelfth century. It collapsed in 1350 and was replaced with the present church, which was consecrated in 1352 and dedicated to the Blessed Virgin Mary. It became known as St Mary without Trumpington Gate or St Mary Minor, and later Little St Mary's Church. The college chapel was built and consecrated in 1632 while Matthew Wren, Christopher Wren's uncle, was master. It suffered greatly under the hands of the Puritan Party of the university, set up in 1643 for the 'Utter Demolishing of all Monuments of Superstition or Idolatry'. William Dowsing pulled down 'two mighty angels with wings, Peter on his kneies over the Chapell door, and about a hundred chirubims . . . and divers superstitious letters on gold' (quotation in Murray).

Peterhouse was the first college of the poet Thomas Gray (1716–71) who had entered the college as a student in 1734. Returning as a fellow in 1742, occupying a high room, he was a morose man with an inordinate fear of fire. Outside his window was an iron bar to which he could attach a rope ladder in case fire should break out. One night some students placed a bath of cold water under this window and shouted 'fire!' Wearing only a nightcap and nightshirt he rapidly descended the ladder straight into the bath. As a result of this joke he moved across the road to Pembroke College in 1756.

It was to this college that in 1841 the scientist and inventor William Thompson (1824–1907), the future Baron Kelvin, was admitted. Elected a fellow in 1846, he not only laid a cable across the Atlantic but also introduced electric lighting to Peterhouse, the first college in Cambridge to be so provided. Apparently the engines

*Pembroke College.*

driving the dynamo discharged a lot of smoke, much to the annoyance of laundresses who used the nearby Coe Fen as a drying ground.

In 1347 Marie de St Paul, daughter of the Compte de Chatillon and widow of Aymer de Valence, Earl of Pembroke, and of Denny Abbey, founded her college on land she had bought in 1342. Allegedly she was widowed on her wedding day when her new husband was accidentally killed in front of her eyes during a tournament to celebrate their wedding; 'maid, wife, and widow all in one day' and as Gray said: 'Sad Chatillon, on her bridal morn, Who wept her bleeding love.'

Initially the college, known as the Hall of Valence Marie and later Pembroke College, consisted of a small court containing chambers, hall, kitchen, master's room and chapel. It was the first college to own a chapel. The chapel had been built in about 1355 and continued in use until 1665. In the seventeenth century a second court was added and a new chapel built. The chapel's benefactor was Bishop Matthew Wren (1585–1667) who had been a fellow of Pembroke before becoming master of Peterhouse. Following the impeachment of William Laud for high treason, Matthew Wren was imprisoned in the Tower of London in 1642. During his eighteen-year imprisonment he vowed that if and when he was released he would give thanks to God for returning 'unto Him by some holy and pious employment, that summe and more, by which of His gracious providence was unexpectedly conveyed in unto me during my eighteen years captivity . . . from sundry noble and truly pious Christians' (quotation in Reeve). Released in 1660, he started to redeem his vow through the building of a chapel at Pembroke 'for the Ornament of the University and in grateful Remembrance of his first Education, which was in that Place received'. The commission was given to his nephew, the 31-year-old inexperienced architect Christopher Wren. Built in 1663, the chapel is Wren's first known work.

Much rebuilding became necessary during the eighteenth century. Although a building fund was created in 1776 in memory of Thomas Gray, little was done for about a hundred years. In 1871 the architect Alfred Waterhouse (1830–1905) was, perhaps unfortunately, appointed to carry out the required works and some would say in so doing he did serious harm. At this date many of the original buildings still existed, albeit in a somewhat dilapidated state. He declared that the old hall was unsafe and should be demolished. When all else failed he resorted to gunpowder and eventually blew up the building. Now little remains of the old buildings and it has been suggested that the college be renamed Waterhouse, to contrast with Peterhouse. What has been done is irreparable and would be a travesty to Thomas Gray.

Although the college has been known as the *Collegium Episcopale* and the College of Poets because of the number of bishops and poets that it has produced, there was an early engineering interest. The first planetarium was built by Roger Long (1680–1770), master of the college and vice-chancellor of the university, professor of Astronomy. It took the form of a hollow sphere inside which some thirty people could be seated. When a handle was turned the sphere revolved and by means of holes pierced through the sphere, the audience could see a representation of 'the appearance, relative situation and motions of the stars'.

Opposite one of Cambridge's tearooms well known to undergraduates, Fitzbillies, is the Pitt Press. Printing in Cambridge had been sanctioned by Henry VIII, the first printer being John Siberch, a friend of Erasmus, who was printing books in about 1520. Sygar Nicholson followed him in 1534. The first university printer, in 1582, was Thomas Thomas (1553–88), a fellow of King's College. A syndicate of senior fellows was set up in about 1700 to govern the University Press, which in 1763 under John Baskerville (1706–75) printed a folio Bible, 'one of the most beautifully printed books in the world'. In 1804 the University Press converted a warehouse on the south side of Silver Street into a printing house. Two years before, a fund had been launched in London to provide two statues to honour William Pitt, one in Westminster Abbey and the other in Hanover Square. Considerable funds remained and it was suggested that they be used to enlarge the Cambridge University Press by paying for a building opposite Pembroke College where Pitt had been a scholar; that is, for 'the erection of a handsome and appropriate building at Cambridge connected with the University Press, to bear the name of Mr Pitt'.

Designed by the architect Edward Blore (1787–1879), the Pitt Press building in Trumpington Street was erected between 1831 and 1833. Steam presses were added in 1838 and the press went into partnership with the London printing firm of C.J. Clay, which not only controlled the press for the next forty years but also quadrupled its turnover and added new machine rooms, a foundry and warehouses. The Pitt building was only used in part by the press; it was used as the University Registry until 1934. Following further extensions the press moved to new premises near the railway station in 1963. Designed like a church with a mock collegiate front and Tudor Gothic towers rising from a classical plan, it is sometimes known as the Freshers' Cathedral. New undergraduates mistake it for Cambridge's cathedral; there is none.

St Botolph's Church is opposite the press and next door to Fitzbillies. Nothing survives from the twelfth-century church; the earliest parts of the church, the nave and aisle, are from about 1320. Historically, St Botolph was a Benedictine abbot in East Anglia and became adopted by travellers as their patron. Churches with such dedications were often situated at a town gate, such as at Aldgate in London, so that his benediction might speed the departing traveller, and this church is no exception having been built at the Trumpington Gate. Its bells were cast in 1460 and remain unaltered. Near the west door is the font with an elegant painted Renaissance wooden cover and canopy of 1637. There is a monument to the Northamptonshire Robert Grumbold, master mason, 1721, who, with others of his family, worked on many Cambridge colleges during the seventeenth and early eighteenth centuries. The church retains close ties with both Pembroke and Queens' Colleges.

Next to St Botolph's Church, Corpus Christi College is unique in the sense that it was founded in 1352 by two town guilds, the Guild of Corpus Christi and the Guild of the Blessed Virgin Mary. Unsurprisingly the guilds had a business interest. Because of the Black Death in 1348–9 there had been much loss of life among the clergy and, consequently, the price of masses had risen to extortionate levels. The guilds thought that they could create a college for the education of clergy in order that they could make 'supplications to God for the souls of every one of the Fraternity as he departed out of this life'. The guilds 'being happily married, they were not long issueless, but a small college was erected by their united interest' (quotations in Reeve). The licence was obtained in 1352 and land acquired a year later. Initially a master and two fellows were installed. Additional bequests funded more fellows, and the Old Court, built between 1352 and 1378 and which remained the principal building of the college until the nineteenth century, is still not only the oldest and best-preserved complete court in Cambridge but also the second best in England. The neighbouring Church of St Bene't, St Benedict, was connected to the college by a passage and used for worship, and indeed until about 1827 Corpus College was commonly known as Bene't College and was the last college to be established for almost a century. Its first chapel, of which nothing remains, was built with 140 tons of stone removed from Thorney Abbey after its dissolution; the present chapel dates from 1613.

*Corpus Christi Old Court.*

Although the town had founded the college it became unpopular as it began to align itself with the university. Not only did it own more property than any other college but it also levied a tax on town houses called the Candle Rent. Initially this was levied to supply lights for the guilds themselves; however, it was soon diverted to the services of the college. One-half of the houses in the town were subjected to this tax. During the Peasants' Revolt, perhaps provoked by an ostentatious display of the college's wealth during the annual Corpus Christi procession of the Host, the college was attacked and archives, papers and books were destroyed. It was a part of a bigger movement during which time the rioters went to Great St Mary's Church where they seized jewels and broke open the University Chest, burning the documents inside. In one of the first 'Town versus Gown' disputes the masters of the university colleges were forced to sign deeds that were sealed by their own seals, under which they renounced all the privileges previously given to them by royalty. They also promised to conform with the laws of the Borough of Cambridge, to pay the costs of any litigation that might arise between the town and university and to abandon all action against the town burgesses. Following investigations into the riots two of the ringleaders were hanged and Parliament annulled all the deeds that had been forcibly obtained.

Matthew Parker (1504–75), Archbishop of Canterbury in 1559, became a fellow of the college in 1527 and was elected master in 1544. He was a great benefactor to the university and to the college. For the university he built a new street which he called University Street from the university schools to Great St Mary's Church. For his college he left one of the most important collections of early books and manuscripts in the country together with silver and plate. These he had assembled to a large part following the dissolution of the monasteries. The books include a sixth-century Canterbury Gospel believed to have belonged to St Augustine, one of the best manuscripts of the Anglo-Saxon Chronicles, one page of which is said to have holes made in it by ticks from sheep whose skins, used as vellum, were not too clean, and an illuminated Bible, 'probably the finest English book of the twelfth century'. To protect such a valuable collection he ordered that they be kept under three locks, the keys being held by the master and two fellows. There were to be annual inspections by the masters of Gonville and Caius and of Trinity Hall. Should any of the books be missing the collection would be forfeited to Caius College. Such security has been carried out for over four centuries. The collection may be moved to a new library which was formerly a bank and therefore presumably secure.

The college has a reputation for being haunted. One haunting is associated with Dr Butts, master from 1626 to 1632, who, depressed, hanged himself in his room on Easter Sunday. Some say the kitchens are haunted by the spirit of a poor motherless girl of seventeen, the daughter of Dr John Spencer (1630–93) who was a fellow of the college and master from 1667 to 1693. After being discovered by her father while enjoying a clandestine meeting with her lover, she ran to the kitchen and hid in a cupboard where she eventually suffocated. Others say it was actually her lover who locked himself in the cupboard where he suffocated. Yet more believe the haunting to be that of a student from King's College who came to Corpus to kill himself in order not to haunt his own college. It may have been Dr Butts, or this unfortunate soul from King's, who was seen in 1904. It was Easter time, but the ghost, with a wound on his neck, was seen in an upper room and not in the master's quarters. Later a few students tried, unsuccessfully, to exorcise the spirit.

There was a gallery leading from Corpus Christi to St Bene't's Church that served as the college chapel until its own chapel was built and consecrated in 1613. St Bene't's is the oldest church in Cambridge and indeed in the county, wealthy merchants having enabled building between about 950 and 1050. To begin with it was probably the parish church of an isolated village, since at that time the town was across the river to the north-west. In about 1650 Fabian Stedman was clerk of the parish, the 'Patron Saint of Bell Ringers'. He was the inventor of change ringing and as he was also a printer these changes were printed on slips of paper for the ringers. There is a monument of 1657 to master mason Thomas Grumbold, designer of Clare College Bridge, the oldest college bridge over the River Cam.

Opposite is St Catherine's College, formerly Catherine Hall and commonly known as 'Cats'. Robert Woodlark or Wodelarke (d. 1479), fellow and provost of

*The Eagle.*

King's College and vice-chancellor of the university, founded the college in 1473. (All Cambridge colleges except two have a master; King's College has a provost and Queens' College a president.) At the same time he was therefore head of one college and founder of another. He said 'I have founded and established a college or hall to the praise, glory, and honour of our Lord Jesus Christ and of the most glorious Virgin Mary, His mother, and of the Holy Virgin Katherine, for defence and furtherance of the Holy Church, and growth of science and faculties of philosophy and sacred theology' (quotation in Steegman). While it was therefore intended for postgraduate secular clergy, in time it admitted a few scholars who also performed menial duties, even in 1473 a porter was also a student. Nothing remains of the early buildings and the college has the appearance of a seventeenth-century building with nineteenth-century additions. The site of the former Black Bull Inn, predecessor of the Bull Hotel, belongs to the college. It had been left to it by an unpatriotic former master of Caius College, Dr John Gostlin (1566?–1626), much to the annoyance of his own fellows. They used to raise a toast to 'the unhappy memory of Dr "Gosling" who was such a goose as to leave the Bull to Cats'.

The election of a new master in 1861 caused considerable problems for the college. Five candidates put themselves forward including Charles Robinson and Francis Jameson. Under the rules a candidate was entitled to vote for himself and while Jameson voted for Robinson, Robinson unsportingly voted for himself. Of the remaining three, two voted for Jameson and one for Robinson and therefore Robinson, arguably by his own vote, won. Initially Jameson accepted the result, but soon his feelings towards Robinson turned to hatred. Contrary to tradition he voiced his grievance throughout the university and gained considerable sympathy from other fellows. The college was 'sent to Coventry' and students were deterred from entering; between 1864 and 1877 only eleven freshmen a year were admitted. Robinson died in 1909 and all was healed.

About halfway between Hobson's Conduit and Magdalene College are two convenient stopping places. One, on Kings Parade, is the Copper Kettle, a long-established tearoom. The other, opposite St Bene't's, is one of the oldest inns in Cambridge and former coaching inn, the Eagle, dating in its present form from about 1600. Carefully restored during the 1990s, it is known for its galleried courtyard, early wall paintings, panelled rooms, stone floors, and the American Bar on the ceiling of which American airmen wrote their names and squadron numbers. For decades the Eagle was the local pub for scientists from the nearby Cavendish Laboratory. It was at the Eagle on 28 February 1953 that Francis Crick and James Watson first announced their discovery of how DNA carries genetic information, that is, the double helix, 'the secret of life'.

# 9

# An Afternoon Perambulation

acing the Copper Kettle is King's College screen and gatehouse, and to the
north King's College Chapel, one of the finest English perpendicular buildings,
which dominates the scene. The college was the first royal foundation in
Cambridge, founded by Henry VI, aged only nineteen, in 1441. The foundation
stone was laid in the original North Court on 2 April, not by Henry himself on
account of 'the aier and the Pestilence that hath long regned in our said universite'
(quotation in Reeve), but by the Marquess of Suffolk. Having already founded Eton
College School in 1440, Henry intended that this college receive only scholars from
the school, twelve such scholars being under the care of a rector. These modest plans
were later abandoned in favour of a grander scheme having a provost, seventy fellows,
ten priests, sixteen choristers and six clerks all housed in one large court. They were
to be exempted from the jurisdiction of the Archbishop of Canterbury, the Bishop of
Ely, the chancellor of the university, and could obtain a degree without examination,
privileges which were only voluntarily given up in 1851, when scholars other than
from Eton could become fellows. Its statutes then consisted of a provost, forty-six
fellows, and forty-eight scholars, twenty-four of whom had come from Eton, two
chaplains, an organist and a 'Master of the Boys'. These boys, choristers, were
required to be 'of gentle birth'.

To accommodate his college, Henry's plans included provision for two courts.
The first Great Court was to be surrounded by a chapel dedicated to Our Lady and
St Nicholas to the north, a three-storey building with a central gatehouse to the east,
and to the south and west a hall, library, lecture rooms and chambers. Henry
required that 'at least two Fellows or scholars in each of the upper chambers, three
in each of the lower chambers; each occupant is to have a separate bed; one of the
Fellows is to be older than the others and is to exercise authority over his chamber-
fellows and to report on their manners, conversation and progress in their studies'
(quotation in Reeve). The second court, a cloister court to the west of the chapel,
was to have contained kitchens, a bakehouse, stables, a brewery, a cemetery and a
bell-tower or gatehouse giving access to a bridge over the river. Such a grand scheme
necessitated the purchase of large tracts of land. He cleared a huge area of hostels,
houses, shops, streets, gardens, the parish church of St John Zachary, and, on the
centre of the site of the proposed chapel, the college of Godshouse. Godshouse was
moved and in 1445 Cambridge Corporation granted Henry further streets, common
land, recreation land and quays by the river. As access to the river had thus been cut

off from the town, the king granted to the corporation land to enable a new access to the Cam (now Garret Hostel Lane).

On 25 July 1446 Henry laid the foundation stone of the chapel and building commenced, albeit slowly. Interrupted by the Wars of the Roses, very little had been built by the time of his death in 1461. At the east end the walls had risen to 59ft, and at the west end to between 6ft and 10ft. Despite financial aid from Edward IV and Richard III, little more was done until 1476 to 1483 when there was good progress, perhaps helped by the threat of imprisonment for anyone delaying the works. By 1485 the choir had been completed and timber-roofed, its west end being boarded up. It remained thus until further considerable funds were given by Henry VII following a visit to Cambridge in 1506. Work recommenced in 1508 and new work on the vaulted roof, west door and the four towers started in 1512. It was Henry VIII who finally completed the exterior of the building in about 1515. By 1531 the windows had been glazed and by about 1535 the screen and choir stalls had been installed. Ninety years after Henry VI had laid his foundation stone his chapel, measuring some 288ft long by 39ft wide by 98ft high, was finished. The planned 121ft-high tower was never undertaken and its intended five bells, one weighing 2 tons and said by one tradition to have been taken from France after Agincourt by Henry V and by another to have been given by Pope Calixtus VIII, were sold. Meanwhile, the students continued to live in somewhat shabby hostels.

With its four tall pinnacles at each corner and the two smaller rows between them, the chapel has somewhat unkindly been likened to a sow lying on her back. From time to time one or other of the four large pinnacles has emerged in the morning crowned with a chamber pot. It is alleged that a .22 rifle is kept in the porter's lodge to deal with such occasions (presumably the chamber pot and not the perpetrators). The chapel has inevitably witnessed many events. In the seventeenth century during the Civil War, when learning virtually stopped, Oliver Cromwell's armed men used it as a drill hall. It was somehow spared the ravages of William Dowsing (who destroyed superstitions and religious imagery in the churches and colleges), perhaps due to the influence of Cromwell's friend, John Milton. Clark gives an account of the election of a new provost in January 1743. Under the college rules, fellows elected the new provost in the chapel which they could not leave until they had reached agreement. On this particular occasion forty-eight fellows remained locked in the chapel for thirty-one freezing hours. 'The Fellows went into the Chapel on Monday before noon; after prayers and sacrament they began to vote. Thus they continued, scrutinising and walking about, eating and sleeping, some of them smoking . . . at two in the morning there never was a more diverting or more curious spectacle. Some wrapped up in blankets, erect in their stalls like mummies; others asleep on cushions, like so many Gothic tombs. Here a red cap over a wig, there a face lost in a rug. One blowing a chafing-dish with a surplice sleeve, another warming a little negus' (quotation in Steegman). One of the chapel's more recent acquisitions, obtained in 1962, is Rubens' *Adoration of the Magi*.

From the lead-covered roof, accessible from a passage leading into the space between the stone-vaulted roof, with its small holes through which little missiles can be dropped upon the unsuspecting people below, and the timber roof, views extend as far as the Gog Magog Hills and to Ely Cathedral about 15 miles distant. Important visitors used to be conducted to the outside roof where they had the outline of their feet carved in the lead. Immediately below and to the west lies the Gibbs Building, built some 200 years after the chapel.

Various proposals had been put forward within which to complete the original concepts. In 1602 Ralph Symons was instructed to prepare designs but they did not come to fruition. While further proposals were put forward in 1636 and 1685, it was not until 1713 when one of Charles Wren's assistants, the architect Nicholas Hawksmoor (1661–1736), produced two models. A building fund was started and in 1723 another architect, James Gibbs (1682–1754), who was already working on the nearby Senate House, was appointed and started to work on the western range, the intention being that this building, completed in 1729, should be one wing of a court and reflected on the other side. Sadly for Gibbs the building fund ran out and for the next 100 years the college consisted of only the chapel, its small ancient North Court and the Gibbs Building. The North Court was sold to the university in 1829 and absorbed into the Old Schools.

Between 1824 and 1828 William Wilkins (1778–1839) completed the court by building the new hall, library and provost's lodge on the south side and the gatehouse and, finally, his screen to the east, which replaced a range of old houses that had previously closed the college from the street. After 400 years the court was finished, albeit not as originally intended. The buildings were sufficient until 1861 when further additions became necessary; Chetwynd Court in 1871, Bodley's Court in 1889 and Webb's Court in 1908. The Great Court's lawn was finished in 1879 with a fountain crowned by a bronze statue of Henry VI by Henry Armstead (1828–1905).

The college had great wealth, but because of the privileges granted to it by Henry VI it regarded itself as separate from the university and other colleges and so became unpopular. In the late nineteenth century the radical Oscar Browning (1837–1923), allegedly dismissed from Eton College, returned to King's College as a history teacher. He influenced King's men into believing that they were unlike other men, that they intellectually tolerated only those inside the college and not outside, that they had a much closer relationship between fellows and undergraduates than anywhere else, that they adopted an attitude of liberalism in politics, religion and morals and that they had a total contempt of athletics. His influence was so strong that when in the 1920s a King's boat made four 'bumps' during the May Races a flood of angry letters from former King's men, many elderly parsons, was received protesting at 'this dangerous and most deplorable intrusion of the athletic sport' (quotation in Steegman).

While the colleges all eventually had their own chapels, the university – that is, the statutory governing body behind the colleges and the academic standards – has always had its own church, Great St Mary's. It, or rather its predecessor, had become the university church from an early date, perhaps in the mid-thirteenth century, when a large hall was needed for university business and ceremonies. In 1275 a congregation of the chancellor, masters and scholars was held and statutes were laid down with the pious aim of ensuring peace for the university. The earlier church was rebuilt, the first stone being laid in 1478. Despite donations from Richard III and in 1506 by Henry VII who donated 100 oak trees from nearby Chesterford Park, rebuilding was slow and the main fabric was not completed until 1519. The tower, 115ft high, was started in 1491 and took even longer to build; it was finished in 1608 without the planned capping by a tall spire. 'All church work is slow. The mention of St Mary's mindeth me of church work indeed so long was it from the founding to the finishing thereof' (quotation in Murray). Restoration occurred in 1857 when the chancel was restored and refaced by the architect Anthony Salvin (1799–1881).

Not only was it the university church by early adoption, but also it was a parish church, the largest in Cambridge. It is not surprising that such a building should have witnessed so many and such a variety of occasions. In the thirteenth century there was no seating, only movable benches, and up to 1346 goods were bought and sold in the church. In 1341 during the Peasants' Revolt the church was broken into during Mass. Jewels and silver were seized and the university charters were taken from the University Chest and burnt. Martin Bucer was buried in the church in 1551 and his body was disinterred by Queen Mary's commissioners and burnt in the nearby market place in 1557. In 1606 the college masters prohibited 'the taking of tobacco' into church for use during the Sunday afternoon sermons. Before the Reformation degrees were conferred upon the scholars in the church during a long solemn service that began with High Mass. After the Reformation the ceremony was deliberately turned into a farce. It is said (according to Coneybeare) that the examination of scholars was no longer a serious affair carried out by senior university officials. Instead a senior fellow sat on a three legged stool and made his questions as profane and outrageous as possible. He was known, from his stool, as 'Mr Tripos' and so essential a part of the proceedings did he become that 'Tripos' became the regular name for an 'Honours' examination.

The church has witnessed many changes of doctrine. During the first outbreak of Protestantism the missal was torn up and burnt. When the Puritans held sway, on Good Friday 1643 the Book of Common Prayer had a similar fate in front of a cheering crowd, a ceremony over which Oliver Cromwell himself presided. The vice-chancellor and other masters were shut up in the church for refusing to support the proceedings 'all the cold night without fire or candle'. Afterwards they were taken to London, paraded through the City and incarcerated in an old hulk on the river with all the portholes closed and no air, 'save such as they could suck from each other's breath'. Until 1767 shops stood on either side of the doorway and a fire engine was housed in one of the chapels. To regulate affairs a curfew was rung from as early as 1664 to 1939, when the great Tenor Bell rang from 9 p.m. to 9.15 p.m. in the evening ending with the number of the day of the month. Until 1929 the Apprentices' or Bedmakers' Bell was rung from 5.45 a.m. to 6 a.m. Little notice was taken of that bell latterly.

*King's College Chapel, the old and new university libraries, the Old Schools and the Senate House.*

Opposite is a green court, bounded on the south by King's College Chapel, the old library to the west and to the north the Senate House, the latter two buildings, inextricably linked, being essentially at the core of the university. During the thirteenth century the university began to buy up private houses and use them as classrooms. The first buildings dedicated to teaching were started in the middle of the fourteenth century in a quadrangle known as the Old Schools. Completed in about 1475, they consisted of a Divinity School, a Law School, an Arts School and a library. Regent House, the early Senate House in the north range, was the centre of university administration.

The medieval library housed in one room, eighteen bookcases, eight for theology, four for law and one each for classics, mathematics, medicine, logic, moral philosophy and scholasticism. This room was sufficient until George I presented the university in 1715 with 28,965 printed books and 1,790 manuscripts from the famous collection of John Moore (1646–1714), Bishop of Norwich and Ely. While the original library was enlarged it still could not accommodate all these books. It was decided to alter Regent House and build a new Senate House. The architect and master of Gonville and Caius College, Sir James Burrough (1691–1764), proposed a scheme for a three-sided court, open to the street, with a new library to the west linking two buildings mirroring each other to the north and south. After much controversy this plan was abandoned partly because of a lack of funds and partly because it would block to all the view of King's Chapel. It was 'a scheme that will so effectually shut out all View of the noble fabrick King's-Chapell, that I wonder how the University or the College can bear it; and a scheme so injurious to Caius College, that I am fully resolv'd not to bear it' (quotation in Reeve). James Gibbs modified the plan and built the Senate House between 1722 and 1730. The books were rehoused by 1752, not before many had been stolen, as they were not secured. The Old Library was finally refaced in 1754.

As the University Library is one library entitled to receive a free copy of every book published in the United Kingdom, space soon ran out again. In 1829 it was decided to clear the whole site and build a huge new building facing Kings Parade. Fortunately, after many amendments, the university decided it could not afford the work; the Old Library and the Senate House were spared. Eventually, however, between 1931 and 1934 a new library was built across the river in Queens Road. The Old Library reverted to housing university administration.

This Georgian Senate House is where notices of degree passes or failures are posted: 'a site of honour or scene of disgraceful failure'. Degree ceremonies, held towards the end of June, are based on ancient rituals with the pomp and ceremony of the vice-chancellor's procession, possibly including some eminent personages receiving honorary degrees, and processions of students from their colleges headed by a senior fellow, all in their gowns and robes. Not all, however, is pomp and ceremony; one morning in the 1950s a complete Austin Seven motor car was observed on the roof of the Senate House.

Just behind the Senate House across Senate House Passage is Waterhouse's 1870 addition to Gonville and Caius College, described variously as 'monstrous', 'disastrous', 'ponderous' and 'dominating'. The college was founded as Gonville College in 1348 by Edmund Gonville (d. 1351), a rector from Terrington St John in Norfolk who had permission to found a hall for a master and twenty fellows. On Edmund's death, possibly by poisoning, in Avignon, his executor William Bateman (1298?–1355), Bishop of Norwich, moved the college in about 1353 from its site near Corpus Christi College and St Botolph's Church to its present location. The bishop had intended the college, the name of which he had changed to the Hall of the Annunciation of the Blessed Virgin Mary, for the education of clergy; its first chapel was built in about 1393. It remained, however, a small and poor college until the mid-sixteenth century.

In 1529 a student named John Caius (1510–73) was admitted. He went on to study in Padua, obtained his MD in Cambridge in 1558 and became physician to Edward IV and Mary I. He became one of the most eminent physicians (as well as one of the richest) in the country. In 1557 he refounded his old college, which was by then in an appalling state, buying additional land and constructing new buildings and becoming master from 1559 until his death. Intending the college, now

Gonville and Caius, to be primarily for the advancement of medicine, he designed a new three-sided court, open on one side 'lest the air, from being confined within a narrow space, should become foul' (quotation in Reeve). Anyone who left litter in the court was to be fined and he provided 'that there be mayntayned a lustie and healthie, honest, true, and unmarried man of fortie years of age and upwards to kepe cleane and swete the pavements' (quotation in Reeve). He designed three gates, the Gate of Humility (moved to the master's garden in 1868), through which new scholars entered the college, the Gate of Virtue (1567), through which scholars passed regularly during their studies, and the Gate of Honour (1575), through which the scholars went to receive their degrees. A devout man out of sympathy with Protestantism, he was charged with showing 'a perverse stomach to the professions of the Gospel'. His ecclesiastical collection was burnt and broken and he was expelled from his own college. On his death soon afterwards his body was brought back to Cambridge and buried in his chapel.

In 1868 Alfred Waterhouse (1830–1905) designed the massive block, about which much has been written and seldom in praise, close to the Senate House, so

*The Gate of Honour, Gonville and Caius College.*

*The Great Gate, Trinity College.*

close in fact that one of the gargoyles almost touches it. It has presented a challenge for, as Clark says, 'urban mountaineers'. If they did not kill themselves in the attempt, if discovered, they were sent down from the university.

Opposite is St Michael's Church, which was rebuilt on the site of an earlier church (*c.* 1250) by Hervey de Stanton (d. *c.* 1330) to serve as both a chapel to Michael-house College and as a parish church. Sir Gilbert Scott restored the church, damaged by fire in 1849. During the restoration Hervey's stone coffin was found and replaced. Paul Fagius had also been buried here, before, under Mary I, his disinterment and burning in the Market Square. In 1966 the church was partitioned providing a community hall, the chancel serving as a chapel.

Michaelhouse College, founded in 1323 by Hervey de Stanton for a master and seven scholars, was one of several constituent colleges that went to form Trinity College. Other colleges or hostels included King's Hall College founded in 1336 for a master and thirty-two scholars, and St Catherine's, Physwick, Crutched, Gregory's, Tyled, Oving's Inn, and St Gerard's or Garret Hostels. In its present form Trinity College was founded by Henry VIII in 1546 consequent upon the suppression of Michaelhouse and King's Hall and the amalgamation of the hostels, for a master and sixty fellows and scholars. Trinity Great Gate, where Henry VIII in his canopied niche holds a wooden chair leg for his sceptre, which had begun in 1519 as the gate of King's Hall, was completed in 1525 and became the main gate to the new college. King's Hall had an older gate, King Edward's Gate built from about 1426 to 1430 and which originally stood in the middle of the Great Court. It was moved to its present position in about 1600.

In 1593 Dr Thomas Neville (d. 1615) became master of Trinity and was determined to make Trinity the greatest of the Cambridge colleges. He was responsible for the design of the Great Court. In the north he retained some old buildings from King's Hall and the chapel which had been started in 1555. By 1599 he had built chambers to the east and south, and moved Edward's Gate to the north where he built a hall in 1604 and kitchens in 1605. The fountain was built in 1602 and rebuilt in 1716. Water was led to it through an underground conduit, thought to have been built originally by Franciscans in 1325. In 1853 it was said that a student had installed in his room a bath that was filled daily from the fountain. Neville built his own hall in the centre of the west wing and in the south-west corner, kitchens replaced the old Michaelhouse Hall. He balanced the north wing and King Edward's Gate, by building chambers and Queens Gate to the south of the court in 1597 and completed the court by filling in the gap between the Great Gate and the southern range.

The Great Court is far from symmetrical; there are no parallel sides, the gates are not in the middle and neither is the fountain. It has been the scene of much athleticism. One, which is more a trial of nerves, is to make a standing jump from the top to the bottom of the steps of the hall, a drop of only 4ft with a width of 10ft. A real feat is to jump clear up the flight, even allowing for a preliminary run-up. Perhaps the greatest feat is to succeed in the Great Court Run. Here the challenge is to run right around the court, four corners and a distance of some 390yd, traditionally in evening dress after a college feast, while the clock is still chiming twelve, a time of forty-three seconds. Only David Brownlow, Lord Burghley (1905–81), Olympic champion hurdler in 1928, is alleged to have succeeded. An honorary win was accredited to Harold Abrahams as part of the film *Chariots of Fire*. Other Olympians and record holders such as Sebastian Coe and Steve Cram have tried, not in evening dress and not at night, and failed.

Not content with the Great Court, Neville at his own expense set out Neville's Court to the west of the Great Court towards the river. A three-sided court closed with a wall and gateway to the west, it was completed in about 1615. In 1672 Isaac Barrow (1630–77), an articulate preacher whose sermons could last for up to four hours, proposed that there should be a library that Charles Wren would design as his gift to Trinity. Built initially as a free-standing building to the west of Neville's Court, the walls were subsequently extended and the court finally enclosed during further restoration in 1755. Although it was never intended, the familiar view is from the river. Viewed from within, the roof is adorned with four female statues representing Divinity, Law, Physics and Mathematics, the last being shown counting on her fingers. In about 1780 scholars bribed the college porter to give them four fellows' wigs, which were then placed on the unfortunate ladies' heads.

In the north cloister of the court, Coneybeare describes a door at the far end from the library having a heavy doorknocker. 'There is a fine echo in this cloister and a stamp of the foot at the library end will evoke a sound from the door precisely like that of a knocker. So great a part does the illusion play in human impressions, that five people out of six, when they hear this sound, are ready to declare that they have seen the knocker actually move.' It was by timing this echo that Isaac Newton, arguably Trinity's greatest son, first measured the speed of sound. He went up to Trinity in 1661 and became a fellow in 1668. According to Pope, 'God said let Newton be . . .'.

Another great and remarkable Cambridge and Trinity man was Richard Bentley (1622–1742), master from 1700 to 1742. He was a brilliant classical scholar and mathematician, regarded by many as the greatest of his day, a European reputation that still survives. It was he who built an observatory on Great Gate (removed in 1797), provided a chemistry laboratory and in about 1717 converted the rough marshland behind the college into The Backs. However, he ruled Trinity for forty years with almost despotic power. When congratulated on becoming master of Trinity, Bentley, formerly a scholar of St John's College next door, replied, 'By the help of my God I have leapt over a wall', there being a narrow lane between the two colleges, the Trinity side having a wall. The tradition arose that he had actually climbed into the college on a ladder placed against this wall, the Great Gate being closed. Although he lived above all for his college, for twenty years he never attended compulsory chapel, he quarrelled with his fellows and encroached on their privileges. He was unconstitutional. He ordered expensive additions to his lodge. He was mean, and he raised his salary at the expense of the fellows'. For forty years the fellows, whom he called 'asses, dogs, fools and sots', and who for their part loathed and feared him, tried to have him removed. For forty years they failed despite persuading the vice-chancellor to strip him of his degrees, which later had to be restored. The costly, bitter and acrimonious battles, which did great harm to the college and the university, even reached the Crown Court for which he 'did not care a fig'. No one could actually remove him from the post of master except the vice-chancellor and this he refused to do.

For all but 100 years Trinity was, thanks to Henry VIII and Thomas Neville, and is, the biggest college in Cambridge. For that 100 years, between about 1685 and about 1785, St John's, next door and Bentley's old college, held the title. St John's was 'founded' by Lady Margaret Beaufort (1443–1509), Countess of Richmond and Derby, and mother of Henry VII, on the old site of the Hospital of St John. She died before she could make the necessary provisions in her will. However, John Fisher, Bishop of Rochester, despite opposition, suppressed the old hospital, which had been founded by Bishop Hugh de Balsham in about 1580 and was by then in a very dilapidated state, in debt and with few brethren remaining. Margaret's legacy came into being, building commenced in 1511 and the college opened in 1516 with four fellowships. While the college acknowledges Lady Margaret as its foundress, it actually owes its existence to St John Fisher, who was later arrested, condemned and executed in 1535. He was canonised in 1935.

*The Church of
the Holy Sepulchre.*

The magnificent turreted gatehouse carries Lady Margaret's coat of arms with antelope supporters, the arms of England and France, the Tudor rose, portcullises and crowns. Some at first think the statue under its canopy to be that of Lady Margaret; it is not, but it is a rather effeminate John the Baptist placed there in 1662. The First Court, Fisher's Court, upon which Lady Margaret looks down from the second gatehouse, was completed in about 1520 with a chapel in its north range. This was demolished in the 1860s as being unworthy of so great a college, and Sir Gilbert Scott built a new chapel between 1864 and 1869. With its 164ft-high spire it is more like a large mid-Victorian parish church than a college chapel. The design produced in 1687 by Robert Grumbold must be a great 'if only'. The south range of the court was refaced between 1772 and 1775.

The Second Court, doubling the size of the college, was built between 1598 and 1602 by the architect Ralph Symons and financed by Mary Cavendish, Countess of Shrewsbury. Like Lady Margaret, she too looks down upon her court from the third gatehouse. This court leads to the Third Court, with its library, constructed between 1624 and 1674. The college had acquired land across the River Cam in 1610 on which it had laid out a bowling green and a tree-lined walk. It was the first college to build on that side of the river, the 'Bridge of Sighs' (1831), joining old to new, leading to New Court (1825–31) with its neo-Gothic style and lantern tower, known locally as 'The Wedding Cake' and the Cripps building of the 1960s.

Approaching the end of our afternoon perambulation we find the round church of the Holy Sepulchre, a Norman church dating from about 1130 and built on the site of the earlier Church of St George. It is one of four surviving medieval churches in England with a circular nave, probably modelled on the Church of the Holy Sepulchre in Jerusalem. Unlike similar churches it had no connection with the Knights Templars. The impressive church was much altered in the fifteenth century when a chancel and aisles were built, and in 1841 the Cambridge Camden Society employed the architect Anthony Salvin (1799–1881) and carried out, at a cost of over £4,000, further restoration and attempted to re-create the church's earlier style. The church was closed between 1843 and 1845 because a fixed stone altar was built instead of a movable wooden table; the stone altar was declared illegal and removed. The church is currently a Visitors' Centre coordinated by Christian Heritage.

Passing the University Union, founded in 1814 and built by Waterhouse on its present site in 1866, and the 'nursery' for a prime minister, the afternoon perambulation can be finished in sight of the River Cam at one of the traditional neighbouring inns, the Mitre or the Baron of Beef, or at one of the several cafés under beautifully restored medieval buildings.

*The Baron of Beef and the Mitre.*

# 10

# Backs and Bridges

A fter the perambulations the restful and traditional way to view Cambridge is to take a punt, possibly chauffeured, along the World Heritage Site of The Backs and under the college bridges, which can be taken from either Magdalene Bridge near the Church of the Holy Sepulchre, or retracing the way back past the colleges to the Old Mill Pool by Silver Street Bridge where the river is still, just, the Granta. This bridge was known as the Small Bridge as opposed to the Great Bridge further downstream.

What more can be said about the beauty of The Backs that has not already been said? They have been much abused and much idealised. Once a swamp, a sewer, a home of vagrants and a busy industrial river, words now used include impeccable, picturesque, splendid, delightful, magnificent, serene, superb, majestic, magnetic, stately, placid, unrivalled, perfect, quiet beauty, priceless and 'carpeted with poetry' (in Brewer).

Immediately through the bridge, the river becomes simply the River Cam as it flows below the walls of Queens' College and under the Mathematical Bridge. Allegedly, Sir Isaac Newton designed the bridge to stand entirely through its construction, requiring no pegs or bolts. This cannot be so as it was designed some twenty years after his death by the bridge architect William Etheridge, built in wood by James Essex (1722–84) in 1749 and pegged. As the wood rotted it had to be rebuilt, first in 1867 and then in 1902. It is also said to have been taken apart by Queens' undergraduates, who then found they could not put it together again.

The River Cam flows past colleges that do not lie on the perambulations. The first of these is Queens' College, to which college the Mathematical Bridge belongs and the fifteenth- and eighteenth-century red-brick walls of which rise straight out of the water in which they are in turn reflected. In 1446 Andrew Doket (or Ducket, d. 1484) rector of St Botolph's Church obtained a charter to found the College of St Bernard of Cambridge for a president and four fellows, on the site of the former St Bernard's Hostel, a house previously founded by Cistercian monks to accommodate their scholars in Cambridge. Financial problems forced Andrew Doket, by that time president, a post that he was to hold for forty years, to seek the patronage of Margaret of Anjou (1430–82), wife of Henry VI. She refounded the college, the only one in Cambridge founded at that time by a queen of England, in 1448, as the Queen's College of St Margaret and St Bernard, 'in the whiche Vniursite is no College founded by eny Quene of England hidertoward' (quotation

*The Mathematical Bridge, Queens' College.*

in Reeve). The First Court, containing chapel, library, kitchen and hall, was completed, partly by subscription from Andrew Doket's parishioners, by 1454 and the gatehouse, still retaining the original doors, followed soon after. The Wars of the Roses intervened. The college faced further financial difficulties and Andrew Doket then sought assistance from the new king's wife, Elizabeth Woodville (1437?–92). In 1475 she refounded and endowed the college and gave it its statutes. She became a 'foundress by right of succession' and since that date the college has been known as Queens' College and not Queen's College.

Traditionally, Erasmus is said to have occupied rooms between 1510 and 1514 at the top of the First Court's south-west turret, approached by a staircase from the mid-seventeenth-century Pump Court. Originally built of clunch and stone, it was replaced by the present red-brick by James Essex in 1756. Erasmus's 'labour in mounting so many stairs [was] recompensed with a pleasant prospect round him'. The Second Court, the medieval and practically unaltered Cloister Court, of the late fifteenth and early sixteenth century, with the timbered gallery of the President's Lodge occupying the entire north front, is arguably the most beautiful, charming and intimate court in Cambridge.

Walnut Tree Court, dating from between 1616 and 1618, where it is said there have been walnut trees since Jacobean times, lies to the north, as does the new chapel built by Bodley in about 1890. Across the Mathematical Bridge is the long, curved twentieth-century building, the Fisher Building, built in 1935–6, on the site of the former brewhouse and stables. This building, together with further ones from the 1960s, intrude most unhappily on what Scarfe describes as 'the priceless green of the Backs'.

Passing under King's Bridge, or indeed just about any other bridge of The Backs can be hazardous for punters, particularly those wielding the pole. There are two hazards; either the pole can become stuck in the bed of the river and at the same time jammed against the bridge or those standing on the bridge can grab the pole. In either case the best thing is to let go! Wilkins in 1818 built the present single-arched King's Bridge, some 40yd south of an earlier bridge. Suddenly the view widens with, on the right bank, the sweeping lawns of King's College, King's College Chapel and the Gibbs Building and overlooked by the south wing of Clare College. On the left bank are tussocky fields where King's College School Choristers have played rugby and where black and white cows have grazed.

*King's College Chapel and Clare College.*

It is hard to imagine how the scene once looked. First a swamp, King's lawn is the site of streets, lanes, houses, hythes and wharfs, where in the fourteenth and early fifteenth century boats from King's Lynn unloaded their wares. Henry VI swept all this away in about 1440. Apart from a few barges, the River Cam became a neglected river. As the colleges spread further along The Backs, the horses, which were used to pull the barges up and down the river, had no towpath. One was built in the middle of the river and when Jesus Green Lock was built, holding higher water levels, the horses had to wade through several feet of water to reach the upstream mills.

It was an unsavoury area; there was no beauty. As the common land was acquired by the colleges, Trinity College 'doth commonly use to lay their muck and their manure on their backside upon the aforesaid common green, where they will suffer no man else to do the like and have built a common jakes upon part of the same' (quotation in Taylor). Town and university sewers flowed untreated into the river. It was the home of beggars who preyed on the scholars and their rooms, and even as late as 1819 the Society for the Suppression of Mendicity was formed to deal with the problem, not only along The Backs but also throughout Cambridge. Thankfully all that has changed.

Clare Bridge is the most beautiful, dreamlike, and oldest, of the college bridges. Thomas Grumbold built it between 1639 and 1640. With three almost semicircular arches, the middle of which appears to sink, its piers have been set diagonally. On its parapet are set fourteen stone balls. However, all is not as it seems and do not necessarily take a bet on how many balls there actually are. One ball from the end, on the left bank of the river on the upstream side, has a segment removed on the river face, invisible to those walking across. One ball appears to be relatively new. Coneybeare suggests that during a feud between St John's College and Clare College a 'piratical' crew came from St John's and stormed the bridge. Before Clare could respond the John's men had started throwing the balls into the river. One sank so deep into the silt that it could not be recovered. Some may assume that the bridge was built to enable stone to build Clare College to be delivered to the site. This is a mistaken view as the materials actually arrived by river.

In 1326 the university and its chancellor Richard Badew obtained letters patent from Edward II to house some scholars in dwellings near the old Church of St John Zachery, the new college being called University Hall. Ten years later there were only ten scholars and the hall had financial problems. In 1338 Lady Elizabeth de Clare (1291?–1360) refounded the college, to be called Clare College. It was to have a master, twenty fellows and a number of scholars. It was destroyed by fire in 1342 and in 1359, after rebuilding, she gave it its statutes. Indeed the college suffered a succession of fires, explained by Thomas Fuller: 'A casual fire reduced their houses to ashes. . . . Here, by the way, whosoever shall consider in both Universities the ill contrivance of many chimnies, hollowness of hearths, shallowness of tunnels, carelessness of coals and candles, catchingness of papers, narrowness of studies, late reading and late watching of students, cannot but conclude, that a special Providence preserveth those places' (quotation in Reeve). Some suppose that the college was 'Solere Hall' mentioned by Geoffrey Chaucer in *The Reeve's Tale*. Others suppose Solere Hall was Garret Hostel of Trinity College.

By the middle of the seventeenth century the remaining medieval buildings were declared unsafe and pulled down. It was decided to set back and enlarge the new buildings. Rebuilding, initially by Thomas Grumbold and later by Robert Grumbold, started in 1638 with the east and south ranges, completed in about 1642. The Civil War put a stop to this rebuilding, which restarted in 1669 with the western and northern ranges, the court being completed by 1715. The college chapel, designed by Sir James Burrough and continued by James Essex, was finished by 1769. Clare Bridge leads beyond The Backs and across Queen's Road to Sir Gilbert Scott's New Court (1924–35), built in memory of some 200 men who fell during the First World War.

Among the college silver is a small covered glass tankard encased with silver filigree, of German manufacture and dating from the second half of the sixteenth century. On its cover is a small conical fragment of crystal. According to tradition the crystal will shatter if poison was to be poured into the vessel, known as the Poison Tankard.

Below Clare College Bridge are the intimate gardens, 'the prettiest corner of the world' according to Henry James, of Trinity Hall, not to be confused with the neighbouring Trinity College. In 1350 Bishop William Bateman of Norwich

*Clare College Bridge.*

(1298?–1355) purchased a hostel which had previously belonged to Prior Crauden to house monks from Ely. The Black Death of 1348–9 had decimated the population and William Bateman founded his college, Trinity Hall, with a master and twenty fellows, specifically for students of both canon and civil law. 'They must not be mere theologians but active-minded men learned in civil and canon law' (quotation in Steegman). A long legal tradition was established.

New buildings were started in about 1350 and by 1374 the hall and east side of the court had been completed. By the end of that century the court was the largest of the period. Georgian stonework by James Burrough from between 1730 and 1745 masks the medieval buildings. At the same time the hall was reconstructed and in 1892 further enlarged. The east range was rebuilt by Salvin in 1852 following a fire. The Elizabethan library was built in about 1570 retaining ancient cases, reading desks and a system of chaining books. During restoration in 1929 a tiny eighteenth-century window was discovered in the corner where the north and west ranges meet. Architecturally interesting, it has been left to be seen, although this is difficult as it is so small.

The chapel by its licence of 1352 is one of the first college chapels. While it received papal permission to hold services in 1366, it was only consecrated in 1515. It was a small building, too small to accommodate everyone during the period of compulsory chapel attendance. It was ruled that first-year scholars had to attend, second-year scholars could attend and third-year scholars were exempted. It was enlarged in 1864 and Reeve tells of a master who is said to have given thanks 'for our creation, preservation and all the rest of the royal family'.

Among Trinity Hall men are Stephen Gardiner (1483?–1555), Bishop of Winchester, doctor of Civil and Canon Law and master from 1525 to 1549; Thomas Thirlby (1506?–70), Bishop of Westminster, Norwich and Ely in succession and also a doctor of Civil and Canon Law; the cantankerous poet Gabriel Harvey (*c.* 1550–1630); a certain eighteenth-century Professor Ridlington, who thinking he was dying of dropsy ordered and consumed a whole boiled chicken washed down with five quarts of beer – apparently he recovered; and the MP Henry Fawcett who became a fellow in 1856.

Garret Hostel Lane and Garret Hostel Bridge separate Trinity Hall and Trinity College. There has been a bridge here since the sixteenth century. An early one was destroyed by Oliver Cromwell, as indeed were several other college bridges. A bridge built in 1818 had to be rebuilt three years later and again in 1837 with heavy cast-iron railings, described in about 1900 as 'a tasteless structure in iron'. In 1939, however, it was described as 'one of the lovely bridges crossing to the Backs'. The curve of the present high concrete bridge was delineated in 1960 by an under-graduate of the School of Architecture, Timothy Morgan, who died that year. Built as a gift from Sir Harry Trusted and his two sons, both of whom were under-graduates at Trinity Hall, and described by some as elegant and by others as intrusive, its steep granite finished rise is a challenge to cyclists and pedestrians alike.

Next is Trinity College Bridge rebuilt between 1763 and 1765 by James Essex to a design of a cycloidal curve carried on three arches. Round the corner is the first of

*The Bridge of Sighs, St John's College.*

two bridges belonging to St John's College and known as the Wren Bridge. With three arches it was actually built on the site of an earlier bridge, by Robert Grumbold between 1709 and 1712, possibly incorporating some of Christopher Wren's earlier ideas, which included an expensive scheme for straightening the river but which was never carried out. While it was not built in line with the principal axis of the three major courts as had been recommended, the second bridge, romantically known as 'The Bridge of Sighs', roughly continued that line. It is definitely not a copy of the Venetian Bridge of Sighs. It was built in 1831 by Henry Hutchinson as a covered bridge in a Gothic Revival style with battlements, ornaments, pinnacles and unglazed window spaces, to join the older and newer college courts.

The Great Bridge or Magdalene Bridge, which was spared by Oliver Cromwell, marks the end of The Backs. There has been a bridge here for centuries and it is suggested that King Offa (757–96) built a bridge here and in so doing gave Cambridge its name. After it was much damaged by floods in 1273 the sheriff increased taxes and promised to rebuild it in stone. In the event he repaired it with timber, which was stolen, and by 1279 the bridge was entirely unsafe to cross. The sheriff became even more unpopular by making people pay to be ferried across. At last, in 1754, James Essex built it in stone. This was in turn replaced with a graceful iron bridge in 1823. It was thought to have sufficient merit not to be replaced in 1972, but merely strengthened and preserved.

The bridge's present name, Magdalene Bridge, derives from Magdalene College, the only Cambridge college to be built immediately on the left bank of the River Cam. Buckingham College was established in 1428 by the Duke of Buckingham as a cell of Crowland Abbey in Lincolnshire for Benedictine monks, supported by Ely, Ramsey, and Walden, under the rule of a prior. Distanced from earlier colleges and the early town, it was a suitable home for the monks who were finding it difficult to maintain their vows when confronted with secular priests, and townsmen and women, in their communal hostels in the town. It was the first hall to house its students on site. At the dissolution the college went to the Crown as an integral part of Crowland Abbey. The lands and buildings were granted to Sir Thomas Audley, Lord Chancellor and owner of Audley End House. He had been actively involved with the dissolution of religious houses, and using his monastic spoils obtained a licence in 1542 to found the initially small College of St Mary Magdalene for a master and eight fellows, spelt with a final 'e', unlike the similarly named college in Oxford.

The first court, built of brick-faced clunch, dates from the early hostels, from about 1425 to 1450, albeit refaced with stucco in 1760 (later removed) and restored in 1875. Some original monks' rooms remain in the south range. The chapel was built by the 2nd Duke of Buckingham in about 1480 and much altered in the mid-eighteenth century. The 3rd Duke of Buckingham is said to have built the hall in about 1519. The college has had a reputation for good food and the motto over the entrance to the hall reads 'Garde ta Foye', that is, 'Mind your Liver'. The chapel is in part original, of the fifteenth century. However, it was renovated between 1733 and 1755 and lengthened and restored in the 1850s.

*The Pepysian Library, Magdalene College.*

One of Magdalene College's most famous sons was Samuel Pepys (1633–1703) who had entered the college in 1651 and obtained his MA in 1660. Under his will he bequeathed to his old college his library of 3,000 books together with their bookcases and desks. He had maintained his library at exactly 3,000, discarding one book for each new one he acquired. The college received these in 1724 following the death of his nephew John Jackson and they are kept, as he had arranged them, in twelve glass-fronted cases. The tops of all the books were brought to the same level by appropriate blocks of wood shaped in imitation of their backs. The most treasured part of the library is the original manuscript of Pepys's famous diary written, in shorthand, between 1 January 1659 and 31 May 1669 in six volumes.

They remained untranslated until 1825 when George Neville (afterwards Grenville, 1789–1854), master of Magdalene in 1813, and his brother Richard Neville, Lord Braybrooke (1783–1858), showed them to their uncle, Richard Grenville, who provided the key to the translation. It was given to John Smith who succeeded in translating the whole work and that was later edited by Richard Neville in 1825, 1828 and 1848. There were two other noteworthy sons of Magdalene. The first was Charles Kingsley, who was in residence between 1838 and 1842. It is said he used to climb out of the window furtively on summer mornings to enjoy his favourite pastime, fishing. Not content with fishing, it is said that he took boxing lessons with a black prizefighter, which was considered rather 'dashing' at the time. The other was the explorer and mountaineer George Mallory (1886–1924), who perished on Mount Everest. Mallory Court (1925) lies across the road behind some medieval houses. Benson Court, nearby and also behind the old houses, required the demolition of Fisher Row, one of the last small wharfs and hythes with picturesque little houses and cottages which in the Middle Ages had lined the banks of the River Cam.

So the River Cam leaves the colleges behind, passes modern blocks of flats and reaches Jesus Green Lock.

# 11

# *Towards the Fens*

At Jesus Green Lock the River Cam's character changes significantly. Gone are the punts; in their place are the narrow boats and motor boats that can reach Cambridge from the canal network via Northampton and the Middle Level and the North Sea via the Wash. Although the River Cam is theoretically navigable above Jesus Green Lock, this lock in effect marks the limit of the navigable river. The responsibility lies with the Cam Conservators, established by an Act of Parliament in 1702, consequent upon disputes between Cambridge University and Corporation, riparian owners, bargees and millers.

Their jurisdiction extends some 12½ miles from Byron's Pool through Cambridge, to Bottisham Lock. While, working closely with the Environment Agency, the Cam Conservators are responsible for all aspects of river management including three locks and the haling way (hauling), one of their most challenging problems is the old one of balancing the many, often conflicting, interests, including preservation, navigation, rowing, and angling, walkers and cyclists and occasionally swimming. They were empowered to raise funds by charging tolls on passengers and goods. In their early days they became relatively wealthy and they not only built their own inspection launch, known as the State Barge, but also the Dutch-style banqueting and meeting hall at Clayhithe. A report of 1829 describes the depth of the River Cam as being only 3ft deep. Consequently, barges had to be restricted to drawing some 4in less and a load of 20 tons; it could take up to four days to reach Clayhithe, 5½ miles downstream. To improve matters the river was dredged, two locks removed and Jesus Green Lock rebuilt. By the mid-nineteenth century, however, their income suddenly decreased owing largely to the impact of the railways. The Great Eastern Railway reached Cambridge in 1845, and while the station was built inconveniently to the south far from the centre of the city there were, ironically, plans for a line to continue to York with a station at Jesus Green. By the end of the century commercial navigation had all but ceased, the last being the removal of ammonia from the nearby gasworks. Today the funds for the Cam Conservators are raised from grants, pleasure-boat registration fees and the Environment Agency.

Although Jesus Green is peaceful today, sometimes the site of a Big Top for visiting orchestras or ballet companies, it was not always so. During Queen Mary's reign, when the Cambridge scholars Hugh Latimer, Nicholas Ridley and Thomas Cranmer were burnt alive at Oxford, a King's scholar, John Hullier, suffered a similar fate on Jesus Green. One of three booksellers appointed by the university,

*Jesus Green Lock, Cambridge.*

Sygar Nicholson, who himself had been imprisoned for keeping prohibited books by, among others, Luther, gave Hullier gunpowder to end his torture. 'His flesh being consumed, his bones stood upright, even as if they had been alive. Of the people some took what they could of him, as pieces of bones. One had his heart, the which was distributed as far as it would go; one took the scalp and looked for the tongue, but it was consumed except for the very root' (quotation in Reeve).

Midsummer Common, site of the Strawberry Fair and the huge Midsummer Fair, well known in the past as the Pot Fair on account of the vast quantities of china sold there, borders Jesus Green and lies opposite the university boat houses with their college colours, the sixteenth-century Fort St George inn and the site of the well-known Banam's boat-building yard, now a modern block of flats with its own private moorings and overshadowed by Elizabeth Bridge. During an outbreak of plague in 1630 forty booths were built on the common for those who were infected.

The river flows between the former villages, now subsumed by the city, of Barnwell to the south and Chesterton to the north. In Barnwell small fragments of a once mighty priory remain. In 1192 Sheriff Pain Peverel, standard-bearer to Robert of Normandy, removed a small foundation of six Augustinian canons founded by Hugoline, wife of his

*Midsummer Common and Fair.*

predecessor Sheriff Picot, in about 1092, from its home at St Giles' Church near Cambridge Castle, to Barnwell village and a monastery he, Pain, had built. The priory, with thirty canons by the late twelfth century, was one of the first convent houses in Cambridge and soon became one of the largest, wealthiest and most important in East Anglia. King John visited it often, and Edward I stabled fifty of his horses there. The priory church was said to be some 200ft long. Although it suffered at the hands of the barons in 1265 and was attacked by about 1,000 men during the Peasants' Revolt, its value at its dissolution in 1536 was, according to Speed, £351 15s 4d.

The small church of St Andrew the Less was known as the Abbey Church, a double mistake. Barnwell was always a priory and never an abbey, and the church was probably, according to Pevsner, a 'chapel outside the doors' and not its principal church. It sufficed as parish church until the early nineteenth century, by which time the population had increased dramatically and Barnwell had a deserved reputation for vice. In 1839 Dr Charles Perry (1807–91), fellow of Trinity College, left college life to reform this district, and he built, at his own expense, the red-brick Christ Church. Consecrated bishop in 1847, he became the first Bishop of Melbourne, Australia.

In the garden of the seventeenth-century Abbey House nearby are only a few twelfth- and thirteenth-century fragments of this once large priory. An underground tunnel is said to run from the house to the former Benedictine nunnery of St Radegund at Jesus College. According to Porter it was through this tunnel the Grey Lady, a nun from St Radegund's and whose ghost haunts the house, came to meet her lover, a canon at Barnwell.

Although there was no priory or abbey in Chesterton, its church was a valuable rectory, which in the fourteenth century became the home of the proctor of the Canons Regular of the Abbey of St Andrew at Vercelli on the borders of Lombardy and Piedmont near Turin, to whom it had been given in about 1280. For nearly 300 years the abbey collected tithes and appointed the vicar and there still remains in the garden of the vicarage their square stone-built house with a vaulted thirteenth-century basement, only a fragment of a much larger building. Close to the river is the Tudor Green Dragon pub, and on the riverside is the Penny Ferry once home to the rough watermen of the Cam whose horses often had to wade upstream through the river towing their lighters to the public quays in Cambridge.

To the south-east of the river is Stourbridge (sometimes Sturbitch) Common where in about 1132 the Hospital of St Mary Magdalene for lepers was established. By about 1280 the hospital no longer had patients, and all that is left is its chapel, which was last used for worship in the sixteenth century, after which it was used as a store, drinking establishment, barn and stable. Restored in part in 1867 by Sir George Scott, it remains, according to Pevsner, one of the most complete and unspoilt pieces of Norman architecture in the county. It lies bordered by the busy Newmarket Road and the Cambridge to King's Lynn railway at a spot known as Barnwell Junction, where the Cambridge to Fordham and Mildenhall line branched away. This line, opened in 1884–5, ran around the edge of the Fens and chalk uplands serving villages and small towns. It was closed to all traffic in 1965.

In the hospital's early days King John granted it a fair, Stourbridge Fair, which was to become the greatest fair in Europe. A tradition says that its success was owed to a clothier from Kendal travelling from Westmorland to London and who found the bridge over the River Cam at this point broken. Trying to ford the river with his packhorses laden with cloth, he and his horses fell. Once across the river he spread all the cloth out to dry; many townspeople came to see the spectacle and bought virtually all his stock. Since he had made more than he would have in London, he made Cambridge his market place the next year; other traders were attracted and the fair grew. Quite why he was in Cambridge on such a journey is not altogether clear.

In its heyday the fair is thought to have lasted about five weeks from 24 August, St Bartholomew's Day, until 29 September, Michaelmas. As its popularity began to wane this was changed to three weeks from 7 to 29 September, and changed yet again from 18 September to 10 October. By about 1800 it was a shadow of its former self, by 1830 it only lasted for two weeks and by the turn of the century just three days, of which the Horse Fair of 25 September was the only really busy day.

After the hospital ceased to have any patients the university, despite continued attempts by the corporation of the town to take charge, controlled the fair. These attempts, however, were eventually successful and in 1589 charters granted control of, and profits and tolls from, the fair to the town, the university only retaining a few privileges. As early as the fourteenth century ships came from the Hanseatic ports with timber, from Italy with silk and from Spain with iron. The river was vital to the fair's success and in 1650, when the New Bedford Level and a new sluice at Denver were being constructed under Cornelius Vermuyden's instructions, the vice-chancellor pointed out that any interruption of the navigation would cause considerable financial damage. 'A great prejudice will thereby befall to a great part of this whole nation by the stoppage of the general commerce at Stourbridge Fair' (quotation in Manning).

On St Bartholomew's Day the mayor and corporation accompanied by the vice-chancellor of the university set out the ground for the fair. These grounds had been previously cultivated and by that day all the crops had to be removed or the stall-holders would be free to trample them down. In return all the stallholders had to vacate the site by Michaelmas. If they did not the ploughmen were entitled to carry off anything remaining on the site. The stalls or booths were arranged in rows like streets, each specialising in a commodity: Cheese Fair, Hop Fair, Bookseller's Row, Cook's Row, Mercer's Row, Cork Row, Ironmonger's Row, and Garlic Row. Cheddar's Lane, Oyster Row, Garlic Row, and Mercer's Row remain as street names today. According to the great Cambridge historian Carter, writing in 1753, there were 'goldsmiths, toy-men, brasiers, turners, milliners, haberdashers, hatters, mercers, drapers, pewterers, china warehouses, and, in a word, most trades that can be found in London. . . . Here are also taverns, coffee-houses and eating houses in great plenty in any of which (except the coffee-booth) you may at any time be accommodated with hot or cold roast goose, roast or boiled pork, etc.' (quotation in Coneybeare). While the variety of merchandise was huge, it was here that Sir Isaac Newton bought his three famous prisms for £1 each, probably French or Italian. The heart of the fair was the Duddery where only woollen goods were sold. According to Carter, 'there have been sold £100,000 worth of woollen manufactures in less than a week's time . . . [there were] orders for their dealers for £10,000 worth of goods a man, and some much more'.

Defoe writing in 1722 concludes:

To attend this fair, and the prodigious conflux of people which come to it, there are some-times no less than fifty hackney coaches which come from London, and ply night and morning to carry the people to and from Cambridge; for there the gross of people lodge; nay which is still more strange, there are wherries brought from London on wagons to ply upon the little river Cam, and to row people up and down from the town and from the fair as occasion presents . . . and in less than a week more there is scarce any sign left, except for the heaps of dung and straw, as good as a summer's fallow for dunging to the land (quotation in Scarfe).

The fair was ended by royal decree and proclaimed for the last time before three onlookers in 1933, an ignominious end for such a fair, once the greatest in Europe.

Still to the south-east Ditton Meadows and Fen Ditton border the river. Situated at the end of the pre-Saxon Fleam Dyke, Ditton means dyke or ditch town and thus Fen Ditton is the fen end of the ditch that crosses low-lying land and which started at Balsham some 3 miles away. Indeed, its main street lies on the line of the now flattened dyke. A story is told (in Porter) of a local gardener and former sexton who made drunken and defamatory statements concerning the young rector's wife's fidelity. The case was taken to the Ecclesiastical Court and two years later the gardener was required to pay costs of £42 7s 6d and to do penance. On the due day some 3,000 people turned up at the church. Some had reserved seats, some climbed onto the chancel screen, some clung to the pillars, some sat on the roof, windows were smashed. The service, which started with Matins, was continually interrupted until the gardener eventually arrived. He attempted to read his penance from the lectern in front of the rector and his wife, standing on a hassock so as to be seen, but it was impossible for him to proceed because a riot broke out. Pews were broken, hassocks thrown, windows smashed and the church bells rung. Eventually the crowd departed for the Plough Inn via the rectory where yet more windows were smashed and stones thrown. While a considerable sum of money was collected to pay the fine, it never reached the gardener who was imprisoned for non-payment and was declared to be an insolvent debtor.

The riverside Plough has long been a popular and traditional spot, together with the former tearooms and gardens of the Barn, from which to watch the Cambridge University rowing races, The Bumps. In about 1825 the river began to be used for

*The Barn at Fen Ditton.*

sport, St John's and Trinity Colleges forming boat clubs. The St John's boat was (according to Merivale quoted in Reeve) 'of prodigious strength and weight standing high in the water . . . like a three-decker'. It carried 'a tin panthermanticon containing two kettles, nine plates, four dishes, a canvas table, a charcoal bag, a phosphorous bottle etc.' The London-built Trinity boat, perhaps unsurprisingly, proved to be superior! By 1827 there was one ten-oar boat, three eight-oar boats and a six-oar boat belonging to Caius College. Because the River Cam is too narrow to race abreast, 'bumping' races were conceived.

There are two racing seasons each lasting four days, the Lents and the Mays; the latter are always held in early June. At the start of the race beyond Fen Ditton near Baits Bite Lock, eights are lined up, within divisions, with a gap of two lengths between each boat. They all start together and the aim is to attempt to overhaul and 'bump' the boat in front. The 'bumped' boat has to pull immediately into the shore to allow the other to pass and give it the opportunity to attempt to catch and 'bump' the next boat. If it succeeds it achieves an 'overbump'. The next day the boat that achieved the 'bump' starts ahead of the boat it 'bumped' and so on. Crews making a bump every day gain their oars. The top boat of the first division is called the 'Head of the River'.

In the late 1880s a man was struck in the back by a boat and killed after a St John's crew failed to stop. While the club was banned from the river, it soon returned as the Lady Margaret Boat Club. Since that date balls have been fitted to the prows of boats. Up to 1892, when there were thirty boats in two divisions, there was a boat procession on the evening of the day after the last race day. Decorated with flowers, the eights rowed along The Backs to the Mill Pool where they turned around and rowed back to King's. Here they remained side by side in rows and toasts were made, the crew of the second boat calling for three cheers for the Head of the River crew. They remained seated drinking wine from the challenge cup while all the other crews stood with raised oars. Each crew was similarly toasted and the proceedings were brought to an end with a 'Battle of Flowers'. During the last such parade the Trinity eight was manned by only three men dressed in mourning. On the empty seats were placards reading 'sent down'; they had all been rusticated for their part in a bonfire in Trinity New Court the night before.

Biggin (Bigging) Abbey lies to the east of the river between Fen Ditton and Horningsea. The dull cement rendering hides a remarkable late fourteenth-century building. It never was an abbey or a religious house; it was simply a home, and one of the smallest, of the medieval Bishops of Ely. It was a house favoured by both Edward I and II. The confusing name may have arisen from the fact that these medieval bishops were also Abbots of Ely.

A settlement has been in existence at Horningsea since the Iron Age with continuity from the Roman occupation well into the Saxon period. At least as early as the ninth century there was a large minster church here. These churches housed a large semi-collegiate group of priests and secular canons who were jointly responsible for the welfare of large areas around the church. Partly destroyed by the Danes, it later belonged to Ely Cathedral.

About half a mile below Horningsea on the west bank is the start of the Car Dyke. This was a part artificial and part natural canal that connected Cambridge with Lincoln and York via waterways passing through the Soke of Peterborough and Lincolnshire. In part it served as a catchwater drain intercepting upland flood water and in part as canal to take goods such as horses, cattle, sheep, wheat, hide and wool from the southern Fens to Roman military bases in the north. During the end of the Roman occupation it gradually silted up and by the Saxon period it was completely blocked.

A story is told (in Marlow) of a Cambridgeshire witch who lived in a village on the Car Dyke. Rose Tooley, born in 1835, married, at nineteen, her cousin Thomas Smith. Before long a series of events disturbed the community. No wagon would pass their house; horses would rear and plunge and despite being whipped refuse to move. However, when either Rose or her husband appeared all became calm and they went past with no fear. Then some pigs 'were taken very queer, whirling round in the field and frothing at the mouth'. When a man was called to kill them they stopped rushing around and started to chase him. 'Some foul witch was stirring up trouble.' The villagers did not know who it was until one day some cattle had developed the plague. They resorted to a charm to find the culprit. One villager caught a live toad and held it in a fire, 'whereupon there was sudden explosion and the toad was no more seen or heard'. The next day Rose appeared with her face, legs and thighs burnt and scorched.

A few nights later labourers returning home saw a strange black object floating a little above the hedge. As it rose higher Rose appeared seated on a hurdle and went flying off into the night. The villagers decided to resort to the final test. They tied the thumbs and toes of Rose and Thomas together, wrapped them in a sheet and threw them into the nearby 'witch-pool'. They floated, 'rejected by the water, as they had rejected baptism through practising witchcraft'. Soon afterwards Rose died of exposure and fright. Villagers crowded into her house and a squealing and howling was heard from the inside of a chest of drawers. When it was opened it was of course empty, but the villagers resolved to burn the cottage to the ground destroying everything inside. After Rose's burial the crowd returned to the cottage, locked all the doors and windows and piled faggots and brushwood all around. When the fire was at its fiercest an unearthly scream came from Rose's room and a little black creature was seen running swiftly back and forth until the fire rose higher and blotted out the sight. The devil had been burnt; the village may have been Waterbeach.

Waterbeach, a low ridge by the water, was once 'a Fenne town of large extent . . . having large and spacious commons and marsh grounds as most of the fen towns have, which is the cause that a multitude of poor and mean people do inhabit there, to live an easy and idle life, by Fishing, Fowling and Feeding of cattle'. In 1769 the Revd William Cole, curate at Waterbeach from 1767 to 1770, wrote, 'A great part of my estate has been drowned these two years: all this part of the country is now covered with water and the poor people of this parish are utterly ruined.' A year later the situation had not changed; 'this is the third time within six years that my estate has been drowned and now worse than ever . . . not being a water rat I left Waterbeach' (quotations in Harper).

*Denny Abbey, Waterbeach.*

It was because of such flooding that in 1351, fifty-six years after its founding by Dionysia de Anstey, a small Franciscan community of Poor Clares, previously well-to-do ladies but now vowed to poverty, moved from Waterbeach to the nearby Denny Abbey. Initially Denny Abbey had been founded by Robert Chamberlain in 1160 as a small priory for Benedictine monks, removed from their cell at Elmeney, again because of flooding problems. In the 1170s the Knights Templars supplanted the monks and used the site as a hospital. When their order was suppressed in 1313 Denny passed to the Crown before being granted by Edward III to Mary de St Paul, the second wife and widow of Aymer de Valence, Earl of Pembroke (d. 1324). It was she who accommodated the Poor Clares at Denny and converted some of the Templar buildings for her private use. Mary, Countess of Pembroke, also founded Pembroke College in Cambridge in 1346; she ordered that the fellows of the college should act as confessors to the nuns. In 1379 there were forty-one nuns (compared with forty-six monks at Ely) and at its dissolution its annual value according to Speed was £218 1½d. The countess is said to have been buried in a tomb that had been prepared during her lifetime, over which a lilac bush grew. The land and converted buildings belonged to Pembroke College until 1947 when it was given to the nation.

Some 500 years after the nuns moved from Waterbeach to Denny in 1852, two years after his baptism in the River Lark at Prickwillow, a seventeen-year-old man was made pastor of the Baptist church, Charles Haddon Spurgeon (1834–92), the 'Prince of

Preachers'. He ministered in a thatched chapel on a stipend of just £20 a year. The chapel was destroyed by fire in 1861 and replaced by the large yellow-brick Spurgeon Memorial Chapel. While at Waterbeach it was said that when he wanted to hold a night service in a remote village he would brave floods and storms only to find the chapel deserted. He would then explore the village by lantern-light and secure a congregation by dint of house-to-house visits. After just over two years he removed to London and preached in the newly opened Metropolitan Tabernacle to congregations of 6,000.

Spurgeon might not have approved of an old May Day custom, described by Harper, when young women collected materials for a garland: ribbons, flowers, silver spoons and a silver tankard would be suspended in the middle. Meanwhile the young men collected emblems of their esteem or disapproval of these young women. 'Then woe betide the girl of loose habits, the slattern and the scold, for while the young woman who had been foremost in the dance or whose amiable manners entitled her to esteem, had a large branch or tree of whitethorn planted by her cottage door, the girl of loose manners had a blackthorn at hers.' The slattern's emblem was an elder tree and the scold's a bunch of nettles tied to her door latch. During the night the men had suspended the garland in the middle of the street. After midday there was dancing 'for the virtuous and industrious, while the recipients of blackthorn, elders, and nettles sat in the cold shade of neglect and resolved to be more objectionable than ever'.

Close to Waterbeach Barracks, completed in 1941 and used variously for bombers, fighters, training, transport command and after flying ceased in the 1960s by RAF Construction and latterly the Royal Engineers, is Bottisham Lock. Here the River Cam enters the real Fenland and its jurisdiction passes to the Environment Agency and the Internal Drainage Boards.

*Bottisham Lock.*

# 12

# The Cam Crosses Fenland

Below Bottisham Lock the nature of the River Cam changes dramatically. It becomes an embanked river, sometimes artificial, as it crosses the lower-lying fenland. Almost immediately Bottisham Lode, the first of a unique series of waterways that include Reach Lode, Burwell Lode and Wicken Lode, joins the river from the east. Some say that these lodes, lode being a medieval word for waterway, were built as boundary markers or as extensions of the upland dykes and defences. It is more likely, however, that they were built by the Romans as transport canals from the Rivers Ouse and Cam across the Fens to the fen-edge villages. Not only did they act as transport canals but they also carried water from the chalk uplands to the east across the Fens, which in turn they drained.

During the seventeenth and eighteenth centuries there was extensive commercial use that only declined with the coming of the railways in the 1880s. By acting as a means of fen drainage, they almost contributed to their own end. As the fenland was drained the land sank and initially the lodes were maintained as high-level water carriers. Further shrinkage caused additional problems with their maintenance. There was the question as to whether they should be maintained as 'high-level' water carriers or made redundant by a new network of 'low-level' carriers. After much debate it was decided to preserve the lodes as 'high-level', embanked and generally navigable waterways.

Bottisham Lode, once a busy waterway is now shallow and unnavigable. It stops short of Bottisham at the small village of Lode, the inland port for Bottisham. Although there is documentary evidence of the existence of Lode in 1154, there is little to reflect Lode's former prosperity apart from a few seventeenth-century buildings. The majority of the buildings are nineteenth century including the Church of St James (1853) and the village was created as a civil parish as late as 1894. On the edge of Lode and at the head of the lode where barges used to load and unload goods, is a white weather-boarded water mill fully restored to working order by the National Trust and where stone-ground flour can be purchased. In its turn the mill is on the edge of Anglesey Abbey estate, also owned by the National Trust.

Anglesey, possibly 'a grassy nook' or 'the island of the Angles', was first mentioned in about 1212. It was founded not as an abbey but as an Augustinian priory, probably on the site of an earlier hospital, endowed in about 1135 by Richard de Clare, with eleven canons and dedicated to St Mary and St Nicholas. The first prior mentioned was in 1222 and 'at his own expense, care and industry [built from about 1236] almost the entire fabric of the church, cloister, refectory, dormitory and Prior's lodging' (quotation in Scarfe). After its dissolution in 1536 many of the buildings were gradually demolished and in the early seventeenth century the Chapter House and parts of the monks' parlour and dormitory were converted into a substantial building. Further restoration and building works were undertaken in 1861, 1926, 1937 and 1958. In the grounds a complex series of earthworks are indicative of the monks' earlier foundations, many ditches, drainage channels and broad rectangular fishponds.

Initially the priory went to the Hyndes family who left it in favour of Madingly Hall. Among its other owners are Thomas Hobson and Sir George Downing. In the early twentieth century Urban Broughton, who had gone to the United States to make his fortune, which he did by marrying an heiress, returned to England with his son, Huttleston Broughton. Urban became an MP but died before he could receive a baronetcy; his son, who had served with the Life Guards in the First World War, received it in his stead, thus becoming the 1st Lord Fairhaven. In 1926 he and his brother Henry purchased Anglesey, reputedly to be near Newmarket and Bury St Edmunds where they owned a stud.

*Anglesey Abbey.*

Lord Fairhaven immediately started building up his famous and remarkable collection of furniture and paintings, the latter including works by Gainsborough, Constable, and over 750 paintings, both oils and watercolours, and prints and sketches spanning 350 years of Windsor Castle. Not content with his collecting he set about creating beautiful gardens and landscaped park in the surrounding 1,000 acres 'that can compare with the great masterpieces of the Georgian era'. The formal gardens demand ideally at least two visits per year, perhaps one in the spring to see the amazing Winter Garden with its snowdrops, narcissi, and the other to see the herbaceous borders, rose gardens and dahlia garden. The landscaping includes an arboretum, sweeping lawns, glades and avenues with classical statuary, some collected from France and some from Stowe, of lead urns, mid-eighteenth-century busts and small classical temples. When Lord Fairhaven died in 1966 he left Anglesey, its contents, 1,000 acres of land, and £300,000 for upkeep to the National Trust.

Bottisham Lode is fed by Quy (pronounced 'kwai') Water which passes below the two adjoining parishes, united in about 1273, of Stow cum Quy. The name is a corruption of Cow Island and remains of medieval moorings can be seen in farm walls. It was the birthplace of Jeremy Collier (1650–1726) who was educated at Cambridge and became a very high Anglican, almost Roman Catholic in his beliefs. While he fully supported James I he refused allegiance to William and Mary. He caused indignation when in 1696 he accompanied two of those condemned for plotting to assassinate the king to the scaffold, where he pronounced their absolution, as if to assassinate a king was not really a crime. Already having been once imprisoned for treason, he was now outlawed but unmolested. At that time the stage was highly immoral, and it was he who made vice, profanity and immorality no longer acceptable in the theatre, opening the door to honest comedy and drama.

The next lode, Swaffham Bulbeck Lode, leads directly across remote fenland to Commercial End, the inland port for Swaffham Bulbeck. During the medieval period there was a small settlement at the head of the lode called Newnham, later to become Commercial End. There was also a small Benedictine nunnery founded in 1190, probably by the Bolbec family, and of which a few remnants, principally the undercroft, are incorporated in the late eighteenth-century Abbey House. During the seventeenth century, as the nearby inland port of Reach declined, trade grew at Commercial End. The prosperity brought by this trade, which included the shipping of wine, spirits, coal, timber, salt and building and agricultural products, was reflected in some fine early eighteenth-century houses such as the Merchant's House (1711) and the Malthouse, which is probably mistakenly dated 1697 on a (reused) shell hood.

The coming of the Great Eastern branch line from Cambridge to Fordham opened on 2 June 1884 and extended to Mildenhall on 1 April 1885, thus linking the fen-edge villages, soon put an end to the river trade. In its turn the railway line was completely closed eighty years later in April 1965.

Swaffham Bulbeck, a farm of settlers from Swabia, became the estate of the Bolbecs soon after 1066. Holding three-quarters of the land, the moated Burgh Hall, from about 1500, may be the remains of their estate. Swaffham Bulbeck was the home of the naturalist Leonard Jenyns, as he was known from 1800 for seventy-one years, or Leonard Blomefield, as he was known for the next twenty-two. He was vicar from 1828 to 1849 and because he could not, or did not want to, leave the parish for some five years, he turned down the opportunity to travel on the *Beagle*; Charles Darwin went instead. He wrote about the fishes Darwin had discovered, edited Gilbert White's works and wrote a *Manual of British Vertebrate Animals* (1835).

Three lodes emanate from the River Cam at Upware: Reach Lode, Burwell Lode and Wicken Lode. The first, as its name implies, goes direct to the fen-edge village

*Reach Lode,*
*Upware.*

and former inland port of Reach. It lies at the fen end of the Devil's Dyke with Reach Lode appearing as its north-westerly extension across the fens. This dyke was one of a series built before the seventh century to interrupt enemy progress from the south-west by cutting across the Icknield Way.

Built some 18ft above the level fen, Marlow gives an alternative account of its construction and, as it happens, a reason for the destruction of the fenland forests. In a forested land, many, including the fire demon, desired Hayenna, the beautiful daughter of a local chief of giants, Hrothgar. Despite her father's assurance that the fire demon would never possess her, she sacrificed two rams to the fire demon's enemy, the water god. Despite this precaution Hrothgar dreamt that the water god appeared and told him to prepare for a battle because the fire demon had joined forces with the tempest. As advised, Hrothgar gathered the other giants and set them to work cutting down trees to make a pathway. Then they dug into the ground, creating both a deep ditch and high bank. After three days it stretched from the riverbank to the highlands at Mount Dithon. The gods were not pleased and the demon of the air sent a mighty east wind that blew down all the trees of the forest on top of them. Then the storm devil sent a gale bringing hail, sleet and snow from the north. The giants all said Hrothgar should not have opposed the fire demon and as they spoke the rain stopped and a great wall of fire advanced against the ditch accompanied by the laughing fire demon. Hrothgar tore away with his great hands the remaining earth separating the dry dyke from the river. Water thundered in and filled the ditch that barred the fire demon's path; neither he nor the tempest could overcome the water god, the fire died down, the tempest abated, and Hayenna was safe. The great ditch, the Devil's Dyke extending to Wood Ditton (Mount Dithon), is still there as is its extension, Reach Lode.

Its fair, possibly dating from the tenth century, rivalled Stourbridge Fair. Under the terms of a charter given by King John, at midday on 8 January 1201, it has been claimed that as it was given its freedom forever it became a self-governing kingdom. In the Middle Ages tradition gives Reach seven churches and it was said Reach was a city when Cambridge was but a small village. Trade developed and it became an inland port for both Cambridge and Burwell, with seagoing vessels from King's Lynn, handling goods such as clunch, sometimes cut and carved for the Cambridge colleges, stone, timber, iron, cloth, shoes, horses and barley. It is one of only four places in southern Cambridgeshire shown on Badesdale and Toms' map of 1741 with a church symbol. In 1742 the dyke split the village in half; by 1768 it had been cut off and levelled to make the green. A hythe, a tongue of flat land thrusting into the fen and to which barges could tie up, was built between two narrow waterways, which in turn led to small basins at the back of merchants' houses.

Although by the end of the eighteenth century trade was declining it still included coal, timber, wine, spirits, salt and bricks. It further declined during the nineteenth century, coal being the last commodity, and finally ceased in 1884. To the north-east of Reach is Swaffham Prior well known for its two churches in one churchyard. In the eleventh century Swaffham Prior belonged in equal portions to the Prior of Ely, Hardwin de Scalers, gentleman, and three knights of the court of

Reach 'port'.

Count Alan of Brittany. It is supposed that one of the churches, St Mary's, belonged to Ely and that the other church, St Cyriac and St Julitta, belonged to the three French knights. The parishes united in 1667 and they continued in tandem until about 1787.

The Norman St Mary's has a magnificent Norman tower, square at the base, the next stages are octagonal and then sixteen-sided. The tower had been capped with a spire, but the upper parts are now in ruins following a lightning strike in 1767. In 1802 the remains of the spire were pulled down and the church was abandoned for worship in favour of St Cyriac and St Julitta which was repaired and restored, rather poorly, using materials from St Mary's. Julitta and Cyriac (or Cyr) were mother and son martyred, son first, in front of his mother in about 304. While there is only one other such dedication to St Cyriac in Britain at Newton St Cyres near Exeter, the cult spread rapidly in France, his best-known dedication being to a school in Versailles, which became the St Cyr Military Academy. Because of the poor-quality repairs to St Cyriac's and because St Mary's had been maintained in a reasonable state of repair by a local family, all was reversed. St Mary's was once again used for worship, the chancel being rebuilt by Blomefield in 1878. St Cyriac's, now in the care of the Churches Conservation Trust, was left to decay.

The second lode, Burwell Lode, leads to another inland port, Burwell, a 'Spring by the Fort'. Belonging to Ramsey Abbey, the Priory of St John had been established here in about 1100. In the mid-twelfth century, there was a civil war raging in East Anglia between King Stephen and Geoffrey de Mandeville. While Geoffrey had helped the king put down insurgents, he had played a double role for which he was arrested. On his release he fled to the fens, occupying the Isle of Ely in 1143, without opposition, as well as occupying Ramsey, Wood Ditton and Benwick, from where he launched attacks on the surrounding countryside. King Stephen attempted to contain him by building a series of castles around the fen edge, one of which was to be built on the site of an earlier castle and other buildings at Burwell. While it was being built it was attacked in 1144 by Geoffrey, who was mortally wounded. His corpse was excommunicated by the pope and carried to the Temple in London where it remained unburied until the pope judged his sons had made sufficient reparation for their father's sins. The castle was never finished.

Like Commercial End and Reach, many old houses and cottages in the old commercial part of Burwell are gable-end to the road, and their lands extend down to the lode, which had divided to serve canals, basins, wharves and warehouses. Wool was exported, stone was imported. Its huge, 'perfect' Perpendicular St Mary's Church, with some Norman fragments, dates mainly from about 1464 and reflects the earlier prosperity of the village. In the chancel is a noteworthy brass to one John Laurence de Wardeboys, Abbot of Ramsey, who had assisted Henry VIII by surrendering Ramsey Abbey, although it was not his to surrender, and persuading others to do likewise. For this he was awarded a pension and his memorial is described by Macklin (quoted in Cox):

This was to Laurence de Wardeboys, Abbot of Ramsey 1508–1539, was probably prepared during his lifetime, and represented him as an abbot. But before his death in 1542, the abbey had been suppressed and he was no longer an abbot. The monument was therefore altered to suit his changed condition, and the lower part of his effigy was turned over, and re-engraved with cassock and surplice, an entirely new head and shoulders being supplied. The indent, however, of the points of the original mitre can still be traced in the stone above the head-cushion upon which he rests.

Below the west end of the churchyard near the ruined castle are the springs, which flow along the former waterfront to the lode. In the churchyard itself is the 'Flaming Heart Tombstone' in memory of those who died in a tragedy of 1727. They had been among the audience watching a travelling puppet show that was on its way to Stourbridge Fair in Cambridge. So popular was the event that the doors were apparently locked and nailed up to prevent more people getting in during the performance. A fire broke out and over eighty people perished. It was said that an ostler who had climbed into the loft with a lantern to watch the show had accidentally caused the fire. The ostler was acquitted, however. Nearly fifty years later the *Cambridge Chronicle* of 19 February 1774 (quoted in Cook and Porter) reported:

A Report prevails that an old Man died a few days ago at a village [Fordham] near Newmarket, who just before his Death seemed very unhappy, said he had a Burthen on his Mind, which he must disclose, and then confessed that he set Fire to the Barn at Burwell, on ye 8th of September 1727, when no less than eighty persons unhappily lost their lives: that he was an Ostler at the time, at or near Cambridge, and that having an Antipathy to the Puppet Shew Man was the cause of his committing that diabolical Action, which was attended with such dreadful consequences.

Had he also nailed up the doors?

The third lode, Wicken Lode, leads through Wicken Fen nature reserve to the village of Wicken itself. Unlike the other fen-edge villages it was never really an inland port. The parish church of St Laurence, dating from the thirteenth century, perches on the fen edge and behind the cemetery are the remains of an old canal along which the stone for the church may have been brought. Inside is a memorial to Henry Cromwell (1628–74), younger son of Oliver Cromwell. He was a popular man who became governor-general of Ireland in 1658. After the Restoration he was 'allowed' to retire, living first at his wife's home at Chippenham and secondly, until his death, at Spinney Abbey near Wicken.

It was not an abbey but the small Priory of St Mary and the Holy Cross, founded in about 1215 by Beatrice and Hugh de Malebisse (or Malebiche), whose family had come from Brittany and had owned the land since 1086, for Augustinian canons. By 1301 there were seven canons, two to say daily Mass in the parish church, and an

*Wicken Lode.*

almshouse for seven poor elderly men. It became a cell of Ely in 1449, with a prior and three canons, and at the dissolution came into private hands. According to one tradition the prior and his canons may not have been too isolated as there was a secret tunnel from the priory to Denny Abbey and its Franciscan nuns. The present farmhouse incorporating remains of the priory dates from 1775 and is said to be haunted, perhaps by a prior who was murdered by his three canons in 1403.

Wicken Fen is one of the best-known and oldest nature reserves in the country, 2 acres having been acquired by the National Trust in 1895 for £10; the reserve now extends to some 1,600 acres. The land, a naturalists' paradise, has been undrained and maintained as a wetland some 6½ft above the surrounding drained land. A small wooden smock mill, the last of its kind and originally from the nearby Adventurers Fen, was re-erected in the reserve in 1956. However, now it works backwards to help maintain the water levels. While it is not a 'true' fen nor a relic of ancient fenland, it is as close an example of the old fenland as is possible, with a spirit of its own described by Storey as 'timeless, solitary, proud, almost aristocratic'. An early twentieth-century description (in Cox) could almost apply today:

Here we find the peace of the fens unbroken – the swish of the reeds against our barge, and the gurgle of the water make a sleepy sound; ditches instead of hedges cut up the plain; three or four black poplars rustle over a thatched cottage by the water-side; here and there, in the distance, is a clump of willows, a pumping station, an old windmill; the peat cutters or mowers may be at work; barges full of peat and sedge are passing along the lode towards the open river. The waterways divide, a smaller lode turns to the sedgy fen, where reeds grow beautiful along the waterside, guarding from sight the last home of rare and beautiful things, which, almost everywhere else, have been destroyed by man.

Unsurprisingly, this fenland area is full of legends. Marlowe tells of a local farmer, Joseph Hempsall, who was accustomed to walk from his home near Soham across the fen via Wicken to the Lord Nelson at Upware. One evening around Christmas a dense fog suddenly developed around Wicken, so dense that it was impossible to see more than a yard ahead. Despite the efforts of those drinking at the inn, Hempsall set out towards Wicken. 'I be goin' by the way I knows and if so be as any of ye like to come wi'me I'll guide ye aright. But I'll never go by road not if the Devil himself were waitin' out yonder.' So saying he set off alone across the fen and the treacherous marsh 'Big-Bog'.

The intense fog hung over the fen for three days during which time nothing was heard of Joseph. When it eventually cleared a neighbour, Elijah Boggers, who had set out to visit Joseph, met the farmer walking towards him. There was something strange about Joseph who had turned to walk silently beside Elijah. Only as they neared the house did he place an ice-cold hand on Elijah's shoulder, saying, 'Go not in there – my body lies in Big-Bog. As I am now so one day wilt thou be. I lost my life in Big-Bog on the first night of the fog – go to Eaudyke and there wilt thou find my body.' Fearfully, Elijah set off to Big-Bog and there lying half in and half out of the water, covered with slime and mud, was Joseph's body. Elijah, terrified, fled for the safety of the Lord Nelson where, when he had recovered himself, he told his tale.

A party of men set out to recover the body but when they reached the spot there was no sign of it. While they were still searching Joseph appeared out of the blue saying, 'Fear not – as I am now so must ye all be – recover my body from the west side of Big-Bog and bury it in Wicken Churchyard.' The men started searching and, as directed, found the body. They took it to Soham where it was afterwards buried. Joseph's spirit now haunts the fen and will not rest until his body is buried in Wicken churchyard.

At Upware in the mid-nineteenth century there were three riverside inns including the Lord Nelson, which became a popular meeting place and club for Cambridge undergraduates who had walked, sculled or skated to drink and fight with the locals, railway navvies and bargees. Two such clubs were the Idiots and the Beersoakers. Such clubs needed someone to keep control, and to enforce the rules, one of which was under the pain of forfeiting a quart of ale, no one was to say what they meant. An undergraduate of Jesus College, Richard Ramsey Fielder, was unanimously appointed 'King'.

At the same time, 1851, the Upware Republic was founded by a muscular group of undergraduates. Admission was denied to no one who could hit hard and drink deep. There were consuls, a president, a state chaplain, a minister of education, a professor, a champion, an interpreter, a treasurer, a secretary and a state fiddler. It had its own laws and its own money; the landlord of the Nelson held the honorary rank of vice-consul. Distinguished members included the philosophical writer Samuel Butler (1835–1902), the Cavendish professor of Experimental Physics James Clerk Maxwell (1831–79) and Master of the Rolls Sir Archibald Levin Smith (1836–1901).

In the 1860s Richard Ramsey Fielder (1823–86), MA of Jesus College and member of Lincoln's Inn, resumed his role as King of Upware, presiding over the 'Bustle', Upware's fair with its dancing and fighting booths, and where he invented alcoholic feats. In 1862 the Bustle became a rolling fight between undergraduates, local men and bargees; the police tried to restore order but they were thrown into the river.

Richard came from a good family with high abilities but had a gipsy nature, an incurable laziness and an unquenchable thirst. It was he who christened the Nelson 'Five Miles from Anywhere, No Hurry'. He imitated the bargees, going about coatless with corduroy trousers and a red waistcoat. A contemporary sketch describes his thin flowing hair of inordinate length, his long dirty fingernails and the 'far from aromatic odour he gave out'. When boating 'he used to take about with him in his boat an enormous brown-ware jug capable of holding six gallons or more, which he would at times have filled with punch, ladling it out profusely for his aquatic friends. This vast pitcher or "gotch" which was called "His Majesty's Pint" had been made to his own order and decorated before kilning with incised ornaments by his own hand. Among these figured prominently his initials "R.R.F.", actual or assumed, a pheon, or arrow-head.' He would often describe himself as 'more R than F' – more rogue than fool. He would often change his lodgings and would remain in bed for weeks, drinking and smoking. He was given to composing doggerel verse commemorating public events such as 'Lines written for the Tercentenary Festival of Shakespeare's Death' and 'An Ode to the Prince of Wales and Princess Alexandra of Denmark'.

Soon after the bargees had left and Upware had fallen out of favour with the undergraduates, the King 'foreswore sack and lived cleanly'. He died in comfortable circumstances in Folkestone.

Below Upware the river flows between high flood banks above some of the most productive lands in the country, an area of the Black Peat Fens. Here the land is intensively cultivated and is so fertile that it can yield several crops a year, producing a large proportion of the country's vegetable supplies, particularly celery.

Today the River Cam finishes its journey 'in comfortable circumstances' joining the Old West River at Pope's Corner in sight of the 'Cathedral of the Fens', Ely Cathedral, and changing its name again to the River Great Ouse or Ely Ouse. However, it was not always thus. 'There is in Britain a fen of immense size, which begins from the River Grante not far from the city which is named Granteceaster.

*Pope's Corner.*

There are immense marshes, now a black pool of water, now foul running streams, and also many islands, and reeds, and hillocks, and thickets and with manifold windings and long it continues up to the north sea.' This is how the Fens appeared to the eighth-century Monk Felix (quoted in Darby), the River Grante and Granteceaster being, according to him, the River Cam and Cambridge respectively.

The Fens evolved from a complex series of geological events, which had started between 100 and 70 million years ago during the early Cretaceous period, when the North Sea extended across much of Britain and western Europe. Great masses of chalk and clay were laid down on the underlying Jurassic clay and then raised to form an enormous landmass joining East Anglia with mainland Europe. Predecessors of the East Anglian rivers, the Thames and the Rhine flowed east and north across this land, eroding the chalk and forming huge basins, of which the Wash is a remnant.

Relatively recently, about 18,000 years ago during the later part of the Pleistocene period, much of the region was covered with ice. As it melted, the sea level rose by 330ft, and East Anglia began to tilt very slowly downwards and became separated from the European mainland. Sea flooded into part of the East Anglian river basin to form the Wash. The remainder of this basin was poised to evolve into today's Fenland. There then followed a long period of successive events that resulted in alternate deposition of silts and clays of both marine and inland origin upon which trees and plants became established. A marine invasion between 6,000 and 4,000 years ago killed these trees and plants, thus forming the first thick layer of peat. As the sea retreated the trees and plants were re-established again, only to be killed by another marine invasion some 2,000 years ago and to form another layer of peat. This pattern was repeated, to a lesser extent, and although East Anglia was generally sinking and marine silts were deposited, there were occasions when the land rose, becoming marshy, and fresh water silts were deposited. A very complicated drainage system of innumerable rivers, streams, meres, lakes and swamps developed.

The ancient River Cam was joined by a small tributary river at Pope's Corner, which flowed well to the east of Ely close to Stuntney and picked up the rivers now called the River Lark and River Little Ouse. It then flowed north-west passing Littleport and Upwell to reach the sea, which at that time was at Wisbech, together with the River Great Ouse. It was probably the Romans who joined the east and west lengths of the Old West River and the River Cam near Littleport to a river, which started to flow near Hilgay, and which picked up the River Wissey and flowed to the sea at King's Lynn. Until the middle of the seventeenth century this was the principal route of the River Great Ouse, the other ancient rivers becoming silted up.

In about 1630 the Duke of Bedford commissioned Sir Cornelius Vermuyden, initially under somewhat ambiguous terms which later became clarified, namely to enable all-year-round farming in the fens, that is, without significant flooding. To this end he built between 1631 and 1651 the Old Bedford River, the New Bedford River and a new sluice at Denver, thus directing the River Great Ouse at Earith directly to the sea at King's Lynn via Denver; there is generally little or no water introduced from the Great Ouse into the Old West River. Nevertheless the river from Pope's Corner retains the name Great Ouse, or Ely Ouse, to distinguish it from the Great Ouse or Bedford Ouse upstream of Earith. Arguably it would be more appropriate to call the river in its entirety to the sea theRiver Cam.

As to the future of the River Cam, it may indeed turn again into a complex river system as it flows after Cambridge to the sea. East Anglia continues to sink, sea levels rise, river gradients decrease, more water is introduced more rapidly as a result of both domestic and industrial building and improvements in agricultural drainage, the flood plains are being built upon and the Fens are becoming exhausted. There will be, in a relatively short geological time span, significant fluvial and marine inundations of this land and the cycle of inundations and dry periods will continue.

For the present, however, the journey along the River Cam finishes at Pope's Corner in sight of the Great Ship of the Fens, Ely Cathedral.

# Sources, References, and Further Reading

The author gratefully acknowledges the authors of the following publications and maps, which have been used extensively as sources and references while researching the background to this book.

Ayto, J. and Crofton, I., *Brewer's Britain and Ireland*, Weidenfeld and Nicolson, 2005

Barwell, N., *Cambridge*, Blackie & Son, 1910

Bloom, A., *The Skaters of the Fens*, Heffer, 1958

Branch Johnson, W., *Hertfordshire*, Batsford, 1970

Britton, J. and Brayley E.W., *The Beauties of England and Wales*, n.d.

Burke, J., *English Villages*, Batsford, 1975

Burton, A., *The Shell Book of Curious Britain*, David & Charles, 1982

Caxton Historical Society, *Caxton Memorabilia*, Caxton Historical Society, 2000

Clark, R., *Cambridgeshire*, Pimlico, 1996

Collard, G., 'The Way We Were', *Linton News*, July 2005

Coneybeare, E., *Highways and Byways in Cambridge and Ely*, Macmillan, 1910

Cook, O., *Cambridgeshire*, Blackie & Son, 1953

Cox, C., *Cambridgeshire*, Methuen, 1914

Crouch, M., *Essex*, Batsford, 1969

Cussler. C., *Trojan Odyssey*, Penguin, 2004

Darby, H.C., *The Changing Fenland*, Cambridge, 1983

——, *The Medieval Fenland*, Cambridge, 1940

Dibbs, J.M., *Duxford, Airfield of Dreams*, Airlife Publishing, 1992

Eltisley Millennium Committee, *The Eltisley Millennium Book 2000 AD*, Eltisley Millennium Committee, 2000

Ennion, E.A.R., *Cambridgeshire*, Hale, 1951

Fleming, L. and Gore, A., *The English Garden*, Michael Joseph, 1979

Galloway, B., *A History of Cambridgeshire*, Phillimore, 1983

Garmondsway, G.N. (trans.), The Anglo-Saxon Chronicles, Dent, 1953

Hadfield, J. (ed.), *The Shell Book of English Villages*, Michael Joseph, 1980

Harper, C.G., *The Cambridge, Ely and King's Lynn Road*, Chapman & Hall, 1902

Harris, L.E., *Vermuyden and the Fens*, Cleaver-Hume Press, 1953

Hawkes, J., *The Shell Guide to Archaeology*, Michael Joseph, 1986

Healey, R.M., *Hertfordshire*, Faber & Faber, 1982

Henderson, R., *A History of King's College Choir School, Cambridge*, King's College Choir School, 1981

Hollis, S. and Moore, D., *The Gardens of England and Wales*, Andre Deutsch, 1989

Hughes, T., M. and M.C., *Cambridgeshire*, Cambridgeshire University Press, 1909

Hunt, P. (ed.), *The Shell Gardens Book*, Phoenix Rainbird, 1964

Hunter Blair, A., *A Level Country*, John Nickalls Publications, 2003

——, *The Hydrology of the River Cam*, unpublished thesis, Queen's University Belfast, 1965

——, *The River Great Ouse and Tributaries*, Imray Laurie Norie & Wilson, 2000

Hunter Blair, P., *Roman Britain and Early England*, Nelson, 1963

Jeevar, P., *Curiosities of Rural Cambridgeshire*, Oleander Press, 1977

Jenkins, S., *England's Thousand Best Churches*, Allen Lane, Penguin, 1999

——, *England's Thousand Best Houses*, Allen Lane, Penguin, 2003

Jenner, M., *The Architectural Heritage of Britain & Ireland*, Michael Joseph, 1993

Joby, R.S., *Forgotten Railways of East Anglia*, David & Charles, 1977

Keesey, W.M., *Cambridge, A Sketch Book*, A. & C. Black, n.d.

Manning, S.A., *Portrait of Cambridgeshire*, Hale, 1978

Marlowe, C., *Legends of the Fenland People*, Cecil Palmer, 1926

Mee, A., *Cambridgeshire*, Hodder & Stoughton, 1965

Miller, S.H. and Skertchly, S.B.J., *The Fenland Past and Present*, Longmans, Green and Co., 1878

Morgan, B., 'Conflict and the River Cam', *Waterways World*, 1996

Muir, R., *The Shell Guide to Reading the Landscape*, Michael Joseph, 1981

Murray, J., *Hand-book for Essex, Suffolk, Norfolk, and Cambridgeshire*, John Murray, 1892

Oxford University Press, *The Concise Dictionary of National Biography*, Oxford University Press, 1997

Palmer, W.M., *Notes on Cambridgeshire Villages, No. 2*, Caxton, 1927

Parker, A.K. and Pye, D., *The Fenland*, David & Charles, 1976

Pevsner, N., *The Buildings of England, Cambridgeshire*, Penguin, 1962

Pipe, J., *Port on the Alde*, Snape Maltings, Snape, 2004

Porter, E., *Cambridgeshire Customs and Folklore*, Routledge & Kegan Paul, 1969

Raverat, G., *Period Piece*, Faber & Faber, 1952

Reeve, F.A., *Cambridge*, Batsford, 1964

Rouse, M., *A View into Cambridgeshire*, Dalton, 1974

Scarfe, N., *Cambridgeshire*, Faber & Faber, 1983

——, *Essex*, Faber & Faber, 1968

Smith, D., *Antique Maps of the British Isles*, Batsford, 1982

Steegman, J., *Cambridge*, Batsford, 1940

Stokes, H.P., *The Medieval Hostels of the University of Cambridge*, Cambridge Antiquarian Society, Octavo Publications, 1924

Storey, E., *Call it a Summer Country*, Hale, 1978

Stubbs, C.W., *Historical Memorials of Ely Cathedral*, Dent, 1897

Talbot, R. and Whiteman, R., *East Anglia and the Fens*, Cassell Paperbacks, 2002

Taylor, A., *Cambridge, The Hidden History*, Tempus, 1999

Taylor, C., *The Cambridgeshire Landscape*, Hodder & Stoughton, 1973

Thomas, W.B., *Hertfordshire*, Hale, 1950

Tibbs, R., *Fenland River*, Dalton, 1969

Warren, C.H., *Essex*, Hale, 1950

Wedgewood, I., *Fenland Rivers*, Rich and Cowan, 1936

Whitehouse, P. and Thomas, D. St J., *LNER 150*, David & Charles, 1989

Williamson. R.R., *Ackermann's Cambridge*, Penguin, 1951

Women's Institute, *The Cambridgeshire Village Book*, Cambridgeshire Federations of Women's Institutes, 1999